Na... ...e to
T... ...KE
DISTRICT

Cumbria & North Lancashire

CLIFF WALLER

Contents

3 **Introduction**
4 **Habitat Map of Cumbria**
6 **Habitat Map of North Lancashire**
7 **Geology and Climate**
10 **Mountains and Uplands**
14 **Moorland and Blanket Bog**
17 **Limestone Country**
20 **Woodlands**
24 **Lakes, Rivers and Wetlands**
28 **The Coast**
31 **Farmland**

Common Species of the Countryside and Seashore
33 Introduction
34 Birds
54 Mammals
57 Wild Flowers
79 Butterflies
83 Seashore
89 Trees

Places to Visit
97 Introduction
98 Cumbria
104 Cumbria-Lake District National Park
112 Lancashire

118 **Conservation**
119 **Hill Safety/ Useful Addresses**
120 **Further Reading**
121 **Index**
126 **Acknowledgements: Photographers and Artists**

Cover photographs:
Top: Red Deer, Dipper, Grass of Parnassus
Centre: Raven, Purple Saxifrage, Mountain Ringlet
Bottom: Derwent Water
Title page photograph *(page 1):* Wast Water

Edited by Helen Gilks and Andy Gillham

Series Editor: Karen Goaman

Designed by David Bennett

The editor wishes to thank Anna Makowiecka for help in the editorial production of this book, Mary Fane for picture research, and Miss J. Ketchen for helpful advice at all times.

The author and publishers wish to thank the following people and organisations for their help: Cumbria County Council, Cumbria Naturalists' Trust, Forestry Commission, Claire Gillham, Lake District National Park Authorities, Lancashire County Council, Lancashire Naturalists' Trust, Miss J London, National Trust, Nature Conservancy Council, North West Water Authority, Royal Society for the Protection of Birds, Miss M Spindler, Yorkshire Dales National Park Authorities.

Most of the illustrations in the section on pages 33–96, Common Species of the Countryside and Seashore, have been previously published in the Usborne Spotter's Guides series.

First published in 1981 by
Usborne Publishing Limited
20 Garrick Street, London WC2

Printed and bound in Great Britain by
Fakenham Press Limited, Fakenham, Norfolk

Introduction

The diverse scenery of the Lake District includes England's highest mountains and largest lakes. On the high crags, Peregrine and Raven occur, and a wealth of alpine plants may be found. Red Deer and Red Squirrel have strongholds in the Forest of Grizedale, and the lakes themselves provide breeding and wintering sites for a wide range of waterfowl.

To the east and south of Lakeland lie the Pennines, a contrasting upland of rolling fells with grassland, heather moor and, in places, blanket bog.

A large proportion of Britain's limestone pavement lies within Cumbria and Lancashire and this unique habitat together with limestone grasslands, cliffs, screes and woodland support an exciting range of plants including many rare and beautiful species.

The coastal habitats of the region have an equally rich flora with fine areas of dunes, slacks and shingle beaches. Cliffs provide nest sites for various seabirds, while huge numbers of wading birds are attracted to the vast mudflats of Solway Firth and Morecambe Bay.

▲ Whit Beck near Keswick – fast-flowing streams or 'becks' carry water down from the mountains to the rivers and lakes.

How to Use this Book

The first section of this book, pages 4–32, illustrated with colour photographs and paintings, describes the habitats and wildlife characteristic of the Lake District and surrounding Cumbria and North Lancashire. There are colour maps on pages 4–6 showing the main areas in which the habitats occur. Many habitats are closely linked to the geology and climatic conditions of the region and these features are described on pages 7–9.

The middle section of the book, pages 33–96, contains illustrations of over 350 species of animals and plants commonly found in Cumbria, Lancashire and much of Britain. Further details on how to use this section are found on page 33.

The third section of the book, "Places to Visit", found on pages 97–117, contains descriptions of over 100 places of interest in Cumbria and Lancashire. Each county has a separate list and a map showing the location of the sites. The places described include specific habitats, nature reserves, nature trails, birdwatching points, and also zoos, country parks, gardens and museums. Further details on how to use this section are found on page 97.

Information such as useful addresses, good reference books, hill safety and a full index are found at the end of the book. Use the index to find out whether a species is illustrated – page numbers referring to illustrations appear in bold.

When visiting the countryside, care should be taken to respect the habitats and the wildlife living there. Flowers should not be picked, nesting birds and mammals with young should not be disturbed, and the Country Code, set out on page 118, should always be followed. Some of the problems related to nature conservation are also discussed on page 118.

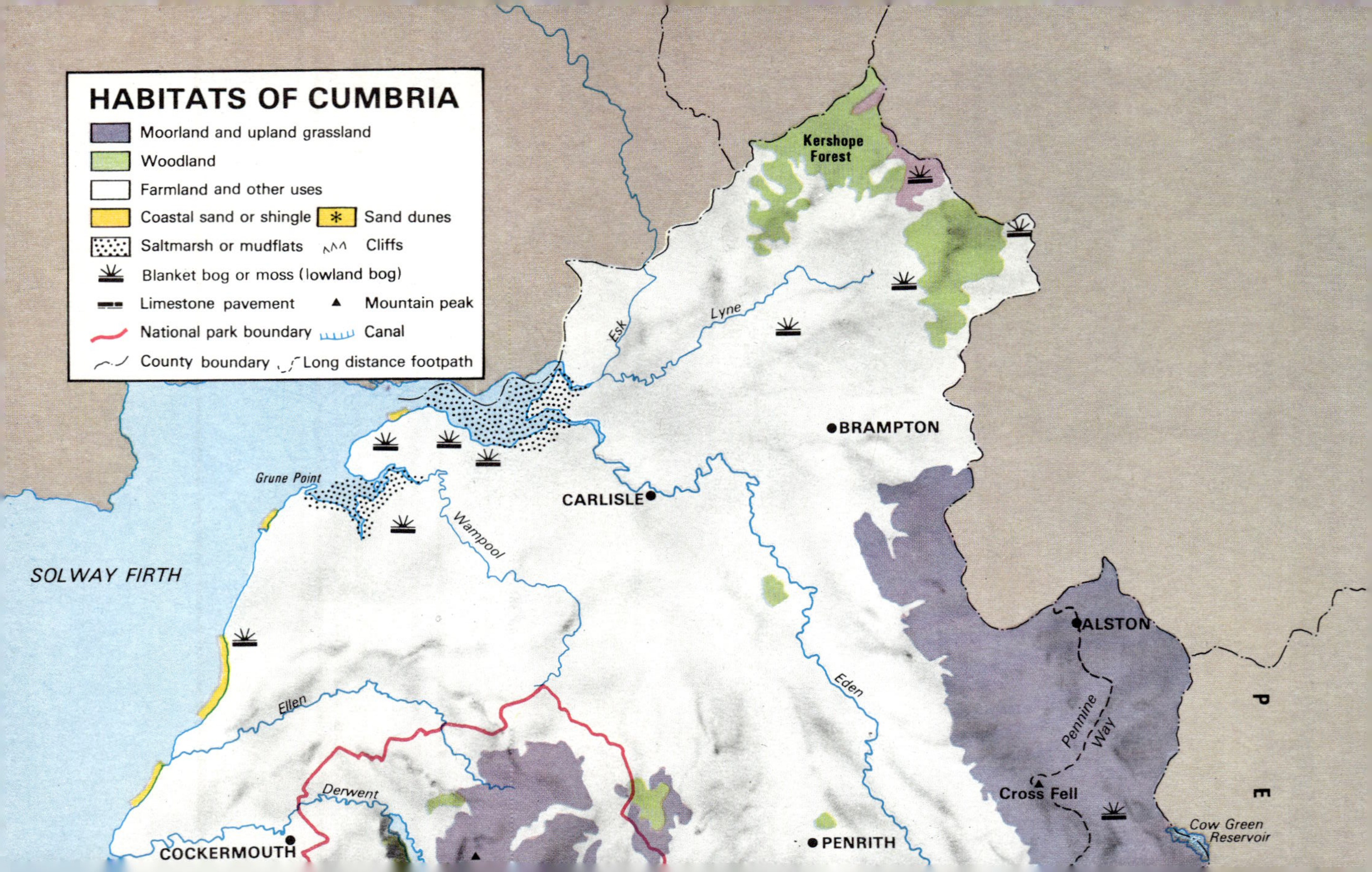
HABITATS OF CUMBRIA
Moorland and upland grassland
Woodland
Farmland and other uses
Coastal sand or shingle
Sand dunes
Saltmarsh or mudflats
Cliffs
Blanket bog or moss (lowland bog)
Limestone pavement
Mountain peak
National park boundary
Canal
County boundary
Long distance footpath
Kershope Forest
Esk
Lyne
BRAMPTON
Grune Point
CARLISLE
Wampool
SOLWAY FIRTH
ALSTON
Eden
Ellen
Pennine Way
P
E
Derwent
Cross Fell
Cow Green Reservoir
COCKERMOUTH
PENRITH

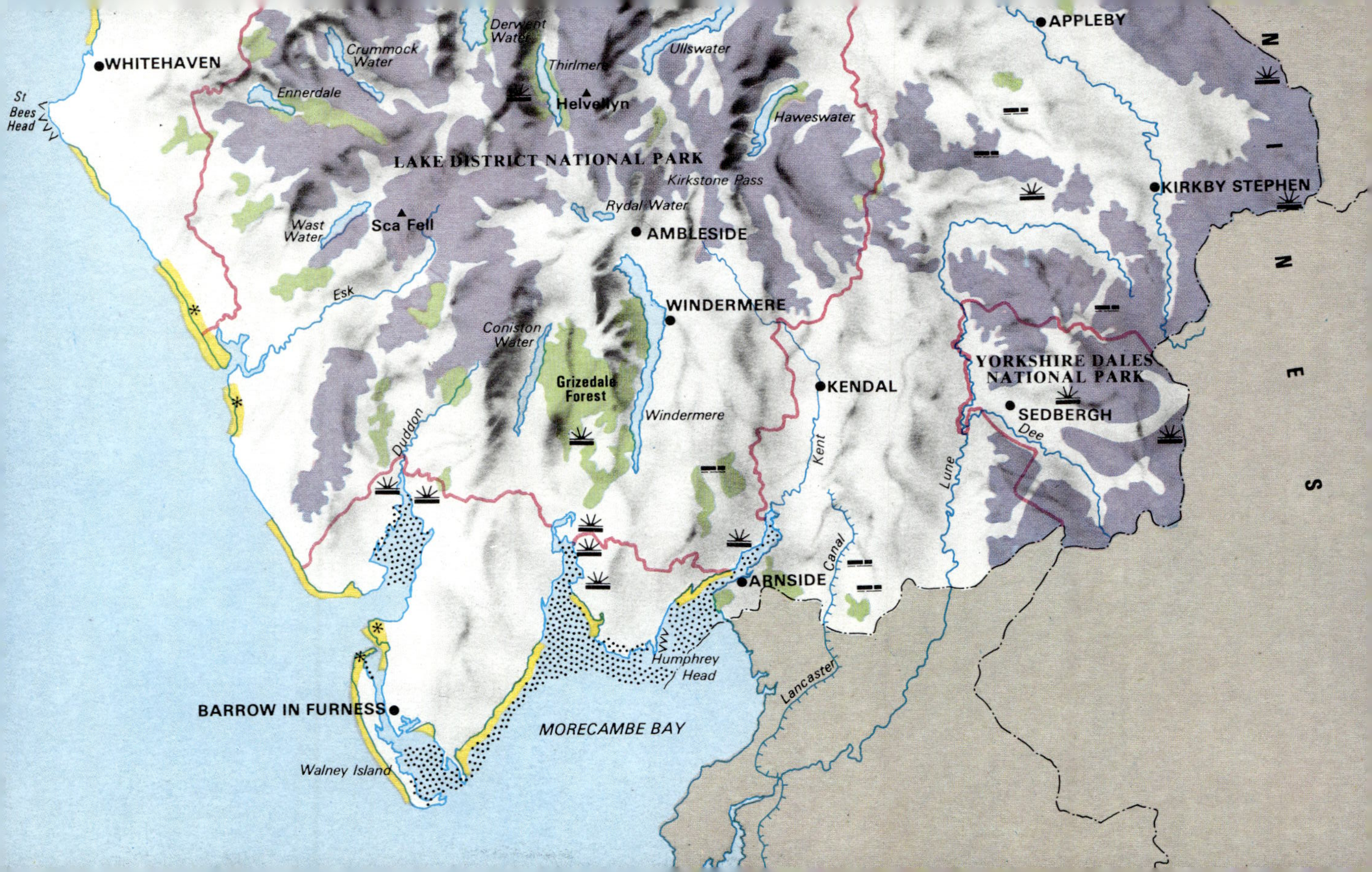
WHITEHAVEN
St Bees Head
Crummock Water
Ennerdale
Derwent Water
Thirlmere
Helvellyn
Ullswater
Haweswater
LAKE DISTRICT NATIONAL PARK
Kirkstone Pass
Rydal Water
Wast Water
Sca Fell
AMBLESIDE
Esk
WINDERMERE
Coniston Water
Grizedale Forest
Windermere
Duddon
KENDAL
Kent
Lune
Canal
ARNSIDE
Humphrey Head
Lancaster
BARROW IN FURNESS
MORECAMBE BAY
Walney Island
APPLEBY
KIRKBY STEPHEN
YORKSHIRE DALES NATIONAL PARK
SEDBERGH
Dee
P E N N I N E S

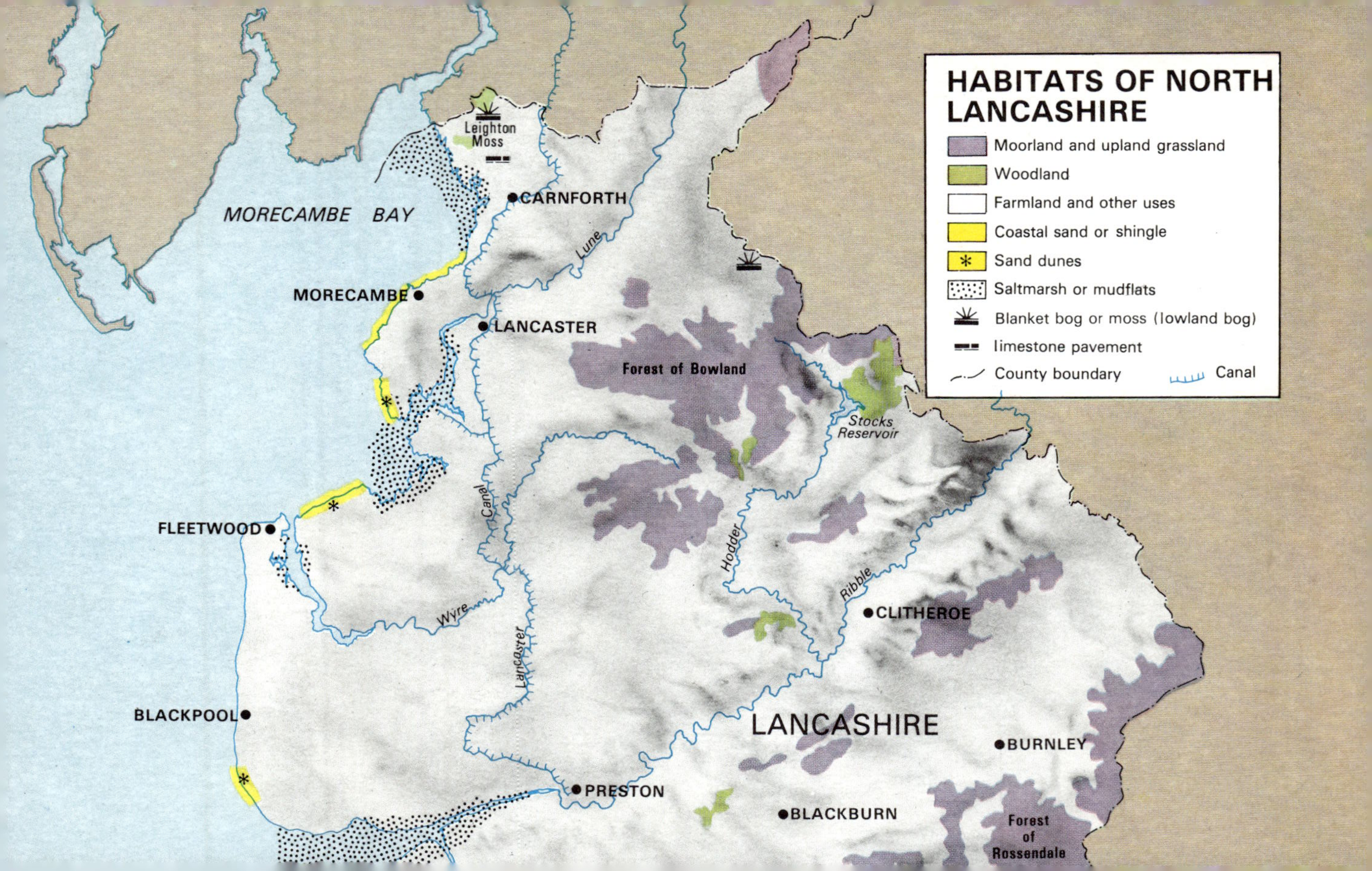
HABITATS OF NORTH LANCASHIRE
Moorland and upland grassland
Woodland
Farmland and other uses
Coastal sand or shingle
Sand dunes
Saltmarsh or mudflats
Blanket bog or moss (lowland bog)
limestone pavement
County boundary
Canal
MORECAMBE BAY
Leighton Moss
CARNFORTH
Lune
MORECAMBE
LANCASTER
Forest of Bowland
Stocks Reservoir
Canal
FLEETWOOD
Hodder
Ribble
Wyre
CLITHEROE
Lancaster
BLACKPOOL
LANCASHIRE
BURNLEY
PRESTON
BLACKBURN
Forest of Rossendale

Geology and Climate

Geological features

The great variety in the landscape of Cumbria and North Lancashire has produced a wide range of habitats for wildlife. A basic knowledge of the geology of the region is invaluable in explaining features of the landscape and why certain species of plants and animals occur where they do. The nature of the underlaying rock generally determines the composition of the soil, which in turn affects the range of plants able to grow there. The most important aspect is whether the soil is acidic and poor in plant nutrients, or whether it is more basic and richer, especially in calcium.

The effect of the underlying rock can however be reduced in areas of heavy rainfall where water percolating through the soil tends to remove the nutrients. Moorland vegetation often occurs on such soils. Alternatively, water draining from calcium-rich rock (for example, limestone) can create a pocket of richer soil in an otherwise acid area. In many lowland areas the bedded rock is overlain by a layer of material such as boulder clay, deposited during glacial times, and so does not greatly influence soils.

The oldest group of rocks in the region are the Skiddaw Slates of northern Lakeland. These were laid down as layers of mud on the floor of an ancient sea about 400 million years ago. Prolonged volcanic activity then caused the sea bed to lift and fold, rather like a pack of cards being dropped and stacked in all directions and angles. In general the mountains formed of Skiddaw Slates are relatively smooth, with few rocky cliff faces, and support plants which are acid-tolerant.

The rocks of the Borrowdale Volcanic Series which occupy central Lakeland are also of volcanic origin and are made up of lava and ash which has been compressed and hardened, some of it into a greenish slate which is used for roofing.

▼ The imposing landscape of the Lake District owes much to the effects of the Ice Ages. In the mountains, ice enlarged existing valleys and carved steep cliffs, ridges and corries.

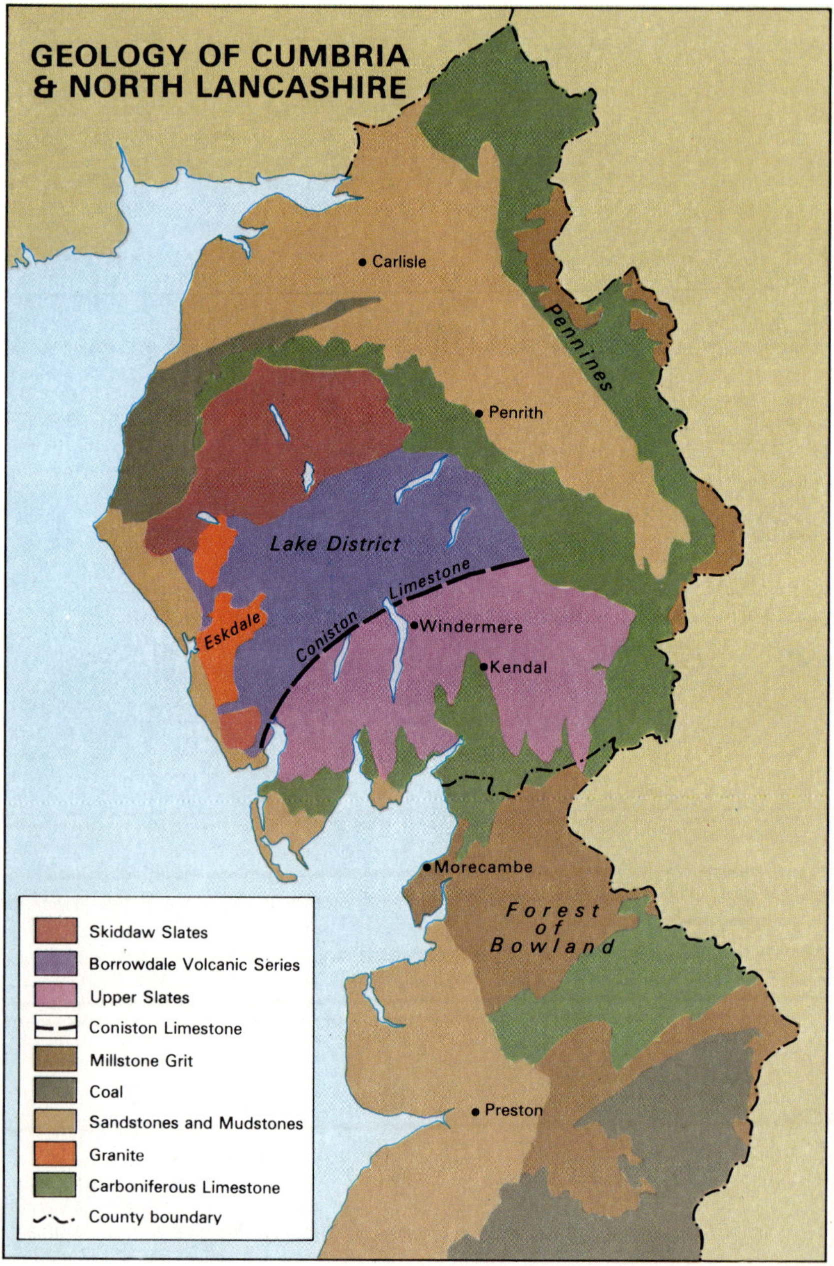
GEOLOGY OF CUMBRIA
& NORTH LANCASHIRE
Carlisle
Pennines
Penrith
Lake District
Coniston Limestone
Eskdale
Windermere
Kendal
Morecambe
Forest of Bowland
Preston
Skiddaw Slates
Borrowdale Volcanic Series
Upper Slates
Coniston Limestone
Millstone Grit
Coal
Sandstones and Mudstones
Granite
Carboniferous Limestone
County boundary

The Borrowdale Volcanic rocks are much harder than Skiddaw Slates, but here and there contain bands of softer, shattered rock. Acid soils are generally associated with the Borrowdale Volcanics, but outcrops of more lime-rich material do occur and often more fertile soils lie in the valley bottoms.

The rocks of southern Lakeland, the Upper Slates, are similar to the Skiddaw Slates but are younger, dating from the Silurian Period around 350 million years ago. They often form what looks like a mountainous landscape in miniature and can produce a variety of habitats within a small area. The rock is mainly acidic, but with some impure limestone in places which, together with its lower altitude and milder climate, gives rise to richer soils than the Borrowdale Volcanic Series.

Running in a narrow band between the Borrowdale and Silurian rocks is the Coniston Limestone. Here and there along its route, soils are sufficiently rich in calcium to support some of the lime-loving plants found in greater abundance on the Carboniferous Limestone (see below).

Throughout the Lake District, but especially in the west, are intrusions of granite, which were forced up from below as molten lava by volcanic activity. The lava cooled to form a very hard rock which weathers slowly to produce poor, thin soils. The pinkish colour of the granite makes it particularly conspicuous in areas such as mid-Eskdale.

The scenery of the Lake District owes much to the effects of the Ice Ages. Glaciers deepened and enlarged the valleys to produce a landscape of crags, waterfalls and long, narrow lakes, often held back by a terminal moraine – a pile of boulder clay and stones left by retreating ice. High in the mountains ice plucked and gouged the rock to form the cliffs and corries (large semi-circular basins) in which can still be found some plants which have survived since late glacial times.

Red Sandstone and Shale that were formed about 200 million years ago occur to the north and east of the Lake District and significant coal measures lie further west. Much of this rock is covered with glacial deposits, producing rich farmland; heather moorland often occurs where the sandstone comes nearer the surface.

Forming a broken ring around the north, east and south of the Lake District and running along the west side of the Pennines and down to the Ribble Valley is Carboniferous Limestone. This rock was laid down about 250 million years ago in the Carboniferous Period, and contains shells of marine animals which give it its calcium-rich properties. A number of rare and attractive plants grow on the rich soils formed by the limestone.

To the east of the limestone area and in the Forest of Bowland are deposits of Millstone Grit, composed mainly of alternating layers of shales and sandstones of similar age to the limestone. Unlike the limestone areas, soils here are often poor and acidic, and give rise to moorland.

Climate

The climate of the region is very much influenced by the westerly airflow from the Atlantic which gives relatively damp and mild conditions. Coastal areas experience warm summers and mild winters, with annual rainfall rarely exceeding 1000 mm. Moving up into the Lakeland hills, however, there can be marked changes in weather conditions over relatively short distances. When the moisture-laden prevailing westerlies reach the mountains the air is forced to rise and on cooling produces the clouds which give the central valleys of the Lake District well over 2000 mm of rain per year. In the high mountains annual precipitation exceeds 3500 mm. In the winter months much of this falls as snow, giving around 106 days a year with snow cover on the mountains and high fells of Lakeland and the Pennines. Long periods of snow cover may occur on Cross Fell, some of the eastern fells of the Lake District, and locally in gullies and corries, but are rare elsewhere. Winters in the Pennines, an area subject to cold easterly winds such as the Helm Wind, are generally harsher than in the Lake District. This climatic difference is partly responsible for the more luxurious growth of trees to be found in Lakeland as compared to the Pennines.

Mountains and Uplands

The Lake District mountains and fells (a local word for upland areas), the Cumbrian Pennines and the hills of North-east Lancashire form an extensive area of wild and sometimes remote upland. Most rugged are the mountains of the Lake District with their steep slopes, cliffs, corries, ridges and peaked summits. They include England's highest mountain, Scafell Pike (980 m/3214ft). The Pennines are generally lower with gently contoured hills, broad valleys and high plateaux; the highest Pennine summit, Cross Fell, rises to 890 m.

Mountain and Fell Tops

On the summits of the mountains and fells low temperatures, strong winds and, in some localities, a prolonged snow cover, produce a sub-arctic climate in which a limited range of plants can survive. Most common on the areas of thin, acid soil is a short turf with grasses, sedges, mosses and lichens. Where there is limited sheep grazing and less exposure, dwarf shrubs such as Cowberry, Bilberry and the much rarer Bearberry occur. On more exposed stony ground the Woolly Hair Moss (*Rhacomitrium langinosum*) may become extensive. Least Willow, a prostrate shrub, also grows in very exposed situations and can be seen at the top of Helvellyn and other mountains.

The most interesting vegetation of the mountains is found in the more sheltered corries, screes and gullies, often just below exposed summits or ridges. Especially where rocks richer in calcium occur and where there is a trickle of water, the ledges and slopes often form a natural rock garden containing alpine plants such as Starry, Yellow, Purple and Mossy Saxifrage, Roseroot, Mountain Sorrel, Alpine Lady's Mantle and Alpine Saw-wort together with three plants more commonly associated with the coast – Thrift, Sea Campion and Sea Plantain. Certain plants, relics of former woodlands, also grow in the mountains, flourishing where there are moist, sheltered sites free of grazing sheep, often side by side with the alpines; Wood Cranesbill, Wood Sorrel, Water Avens Wood Anemone, Great Woodrush and several ferns are some of the woodland plants most commonly seen in the mountains.

▲ Roseroot, with its thick fleshy leaves, grows in rock crevices. Its yellow flowers are in bloom between May and August.

▲ High in the mountains of the region, mats of the ragged, grey-green Woolly Hair Moss may cover extensive areas of rocky ground.

▲ Yellow Mountain Saxifrage, in flower from June to August, is quite common in parts of the region, on wet mountain rocks and in flushes.

▲ The rarer early-flowering Purple Saxifrage also grows on damp mountain rocks. It flowers between April and June.

▼ The Ring Ouzel, a summer visitor to the region, occurs up to quite high altitudes. Buzzards may be seen soaring overhead at anytime of the year. Maidenhair Spleenwort and Mossy Saxifrage which flowers between May and July, grow mainly on rocky surfaces.

Many sites where alpine plants grow in the Lake District are rather inaccessible and are best viewed through binoculars, but Red Screes at the top of the Kirkstone Pass can be visited with ease. Some pockets of alpine plants are occasionally found at lower levels.

In the Pennines, rugged mountain features are less frequent, but outcrops of calcium-rich rock are more common, and where there is little or no sheep grazing, a similar though not identical range of alpine plants can be found. Among the more interesting plants of the high limestone areas of the Pennines are Alpine Scurvy Grass, Alpine Bistort, Alpine Meadow-rue, Alpine Cinquefoil, Alpine Forget-me-Not, Spring Sandwort, Spring Gentian, Green Spleenwort and many of the rock ledge species listed earlier. Other plants of the limestone are discussed on page 17.

Most of the animals seen on the high fells would be more commonly found at lower levels, but characteristic of the mountains are some exciting birds. Raven and the magnificent Peregrine nest on remote cliff faces as does the common Kestrel. Buzzard and occasionally the very rare Golden Eagle may be seen soaring over the mountains. Ring Ouzels inhabit some of the screes and Dippers follow streams up to quite a height. Swifts dart low over the high summits on summer days, whilst in winter Snow Buntings may be seen. Meadow Pipit is the most common nesting bird on the fells, and on areas of short grassland, the Wheatear also occurs. Golden Plovers breed over much of the Pennines and the rare Dotterel may occasionally be seen.

Of the larger mammals, the Fox is the commonest. Its earths are even found on some mountain tops. Herds of Red Deer can also be seen above the tree line, especially in summer, but are shy and easily disturbed. Brown Hares are met with occasionally and a glimpse may be had of a Stoat or Weasel. Moles are active at high altitudes and the very rare Pine Marten sometimes occurs above woodland.

A limited number of insect species are found in the high mountains. They include several beetles, spiders and craneflies, some of which are confined to this habitat. The Lakeland fells also provide the only English site for Britain's sole true alpine butterfly, the Small Mountain Ringlet.

▼ Small 'trips' of the rare Dotterel, a bird once hunted for its feathers, may still occasionally be seen on the Pennine fells.

▼ High Cup Nick in the Cumbrian Pennines, an outcrop of the hard, calcium-rich rock, Whin Sill.

▼ After an absence of two centuries, the Golden Eagle may once again be seen in Lakeland. This bird has a 7 foot (2 metre) wing-span.

The Lower Slopes

The lower slopes, which would naturally be covered with scrub and woodland have been established as extensive areas of grassland by many centuries of sheep grazing. On acid soils the sheep pastures contain a sward of fine grasses, mainly Bents and Fescues, in which Tormentil and Heath Bedstraw are among the few flowers to be found. Patches of the tough Mat Grass and Heath Rush are common and Bracken continues to spread extensively over lower hill slopes. A more diverse flora may be found on the basic soils over limestone and this is described on page 17.

The most interesting areas of the lower slopes are those where sheep grazing is slight or absent. On scree, one of the first colonizers is Parsley Fern. This plant is common at all levels in the Lake District, but is rare or local elsewhere in Britain. Juniper scrub and other scattered bushes may be found on steep but more stable slopes, and Bilberry and Ling are found mainly on drier ground. These habitats are important for a range of insects and birds.

A good variety of plants can be found in wooded gullies, which reach up into otherwise tree-less hillsides, and also in flushes, small areas where seepage water is near the surface. Some of the many interesting plants found in flushes include the insectivorous Butterwort, Birdseye Primrose, Grass of Parnassus, Fairy Flax, Lousewort, Marsh Arrowgrass and Spotted Orchids.

Many of the animals previously mentioned may be seen on the lower slopes of the fells, together with some from lowland habitats. Rabbits in particular continue to increase, despite myxomatosis.

▲ White-flowered Heath Bedstraw and yellow Tormentil – two plants of more acid grasslands.

▲ The rich green fronds of the Parsley Fern can be seen on many screes and cliffs of Lakeland.

▲ The Mountain Ringlet may be seen flying over damp upland areas in late June and July.

▼ The magnificent Peregrine nests on some of the remote crags of the Lake District.

▼ The Raven is a bird of upland areas; it feeds on most things, including carrion.

Moorland and Blanket Bog

Moorland occurs over extensive areas on acid peaty soils in the Pennines, in the uplands of North-East Lancashire, and, more locally, in the Lake District. Much of the better moorland is managed as Grouse Moor by burning patches of heather on a regular rotation to encourage new growth. Sheep also graze on the moorlands and if grazing becomes too heavy, or burning too frequent, the heather vegetation may change to grassland, with coarse grasses forming a sward rather similar to that found on the lower slopes of some fells. Many heather moorland areas contain grassy patches and some are extensively colonized by Bracken.

On the higher moorlands, where rainfall and humidity are high, and the run-off of water is impeded by impervious rock and gentle gradients, a blanket covering of peat develops which may support bog vegetation. Conditions in a blanket bog are very acid and wet and a number of specialized plants are found here in addition to moorland plants from drier ground. Ling, Bell Heather, Bilberry, Crowberry and fine grasses grow on drier peat. Plants on the wetter areas include Cranberry, Cross-leaved Heath, Purple Moor Grass, Cotton Grass, Deer Grass (both, in fact, kinds of sedges), Bog Asphodel, Sundew and *Sphagnum* mosses, which may hold many times their own weight of water. Cloudberry, with its large bright green leaves and bramble-like fruits may also be found, particularly in the Pennines.

In the shallow peaty pools of the lower bogs, or where water flows sluggishly into basins or shallow valleys, may be found the trefoil leaves of Bogbean, the floating leaves of Bog Pondweed and Floating Bur-reed, and the erect spikes of Bottle Sedge.

The blanket peat not only supports living plants, but also contains a record of former vegetation. Peat itself is made up of partially decomposed plant material, and can be several feet deep, having accumulated over thousands of years. Pollen grains identified in the peat indicate that some of the plants growing here today also occurred many centuries ago. Pieces of Pine and Birch wood, remnants of forests which

▼ Stretch of moorland near the Cumbria–Durham border, with Cow Green Reservoir in the distance. The bright pink flowers of Bell Heather can be seen in the foreground.

once covered these areas, are sometimes found deep in the peat, and on Moor House National Nature Reserve remains of the long extinct Wild Ox have been found.

The most typical bird of heather moorland is the Red Grouse. Two other birds which commonly nest amongst heather are the Short-eared Owl and the Merlin. The Hen Harrier, which is extending its range southwards, could also become a regular breeding bird. The Meadow Pipit is the most common bird in many areas and is the main prey of the Merlin. The rare Twite is a very local nester.

Among the birds found on the moorland edge are Black Grouse. The males, called Blackcock, are famous for their spectacular mating displays. They gather in groups, often on traditional courtship areas, known as 'leks', where they fight and display by dropping their wings and spreading their lyre-shaped tails, making short aggressive runs at each other. The females, called Greyhens, are attracted to the lek by the display and are then mated by the dominant males.

Associated with blanket bog and other upland wetlands are several species of wading birds including Snipe, Lapwing, Curlew, Redshank, Golden Plover and, more locally, Dunlin. Mallard are often found and Teal occur on even the smallest moorland pools.

Two species of reptile occur on drier areas – the Common Lizard and Britain's only poisonous snake, the Adder. Frogs occur in many bog pools, some of which are patrolled by the blue Common Hawker Dragonfly. The handsome Emperor Moth is common in some areas, whilst the beautiful Yellow Underwing is another day-flying moth which can be seen on moorland.

▲ Bog Asphodel with its bright yellow, six-starred petals and orange anthers, may be seen in acid bogs and on wet moorland.

▲ Cloudberry, a plant related to the Bramble, bears white flowers between June and August, which later develop into red berries.

▲ The Emperor Moth occurs on moorland and wet fens. The male flies by day in April and May.

▼ Cotton Grass can be easily identified when in fruit by its white cotton-like tassels.

▼ Bogbean may be seen flowering in marshes and moorland pools between April and June.

▲ The Merlin occasionally nests in trees, but more usually on the ground amongst heather. It is commoner in the Pennines than in Lakeland.

▲ Any large, long-winged owl seen hunting by day over moorland or young forestry plantations will almost certainly be the Short-eared Owl.

▼ The Common Sundew grows in wet acid areas; it makes up for the lack of nutrients in the soil by catching and digesting insects which it traps with the sticky red hairs on its leaves.

▲ The Red Grouse is characteristic of heather moorland. Plants form the main part of its diet although it also feeds on insects.

▲ Famous for its mating displays, the Black Grouse occurs locally in hillside copses and wooded valleys along the moorland edge.

▼ The Golden Plover nests on moorland and upland grasslands, mainly in the Pennines.

▼ The Adder, Britain's only poisonous snake, inhabits the drier areas of moorland.

Limestone Country

Although a little of the Pennine limestone has been discussed on page 12, a glance at the geological map will show that Carboniferous Limestone also occurs around the head of Morecambe Bay with outcrops in the hills to the north and east. Limestone country is of particular ecological interest because the vegetation of the grasslands, pavements, screes and cliffs contain many rare and attractive plants. Limestone woodland and scrub also have a characteristic assemblage of plants which are discussed later under 'Woodlands'.

Limestone Grassland

Some limestone grasslands contain a great diversity of plants including a number of rare species, some of which are virtually restricted to this habitat. Attractive grasses such as Common Quaking Grass and the rarer Nodding or Mountain Melick can be found amongst the flowers of Common Rockrose, Dog Violet, Hoary Plantain and Sheepsbit Scabious. More local species include Hoary Whitlow-grass, Lesser Meadow-rue, Columbine and Bloody Cranesbill. Many orchids favour lime-rich soils; species that may be seen on the grasslands include Fragrant, Frog and Lesser Butterfly Orchids. Also to be found, though with difficulty, is Moonwort, a mysterious little fern which blends into the grassland. There are some areas of grassland which are dominated by the early flowering Blue Moor Grass; by late summer these areas often look brown and parched. Here and there overlying the solid limestone are areas of more acidic glacial drift where such acid-tolerant plants as Ling and Bilberry occur.

The birds are much the same as in other grassland areas with Meadow Pipit and Skylark being typical. Wheatears can be seen where there is suitable short turf and where there are rabbit holes or stone walls available for nesting. Numerous interesting insects are seen on the grasslands, the more obvious being butterflies and moths. The Scotch Argus butterfly is found in a few places, though it is very scarce this far south. More commonly seen species include the Small Heath, Small Pearl-bordered Fritillary and Common Blue. The moths include the attractive Wood Tiger and the Least Minor which is found in areas where the Glaucous Sedge grows.

▼ Bloody Cranesbill grows on limestone rocks and grassland, and also on dunes. A pink-flowered variety occurs along the coast.

▼ The beautiful Common Quaking Grass can be seen in many limestone grassland areas of the region. It flowers between June and August.

Cliffs, Scars and Scree

Limestone cliffs, scars (low cliffs) and screes are often spectacular and amongst the best places to see some cf the more uncommon plants, especially those least tolerant of sheep grazing. Ground conditions may be unstable, due to exposure to wind and the downwash of water, making it difficult for any plant to gain a permanent foothold. Thus some early colonizing plant species are able to survive because much of the competition found in the open grasslands has been removed. Species to look out for on rocky ground include Biting Stonecrop, Rue-leaved Saxifrage, Maidenhair and Green Spleenworts, Rusty-back and Wall Rue Ferns, Great Mullein. On grassy ledges and cliff tops, Horseshoe Vetch, Hoary Rockrose and a local form of Whitebeam may occur.

Limestone Pavement

Most of Britain's limestone pavement occurs in northern England, with a substantial proportion lying in Cumbria and North Lancashire. Some of the best examples can be seen at low altitude at places such as Gaitbarrows National Nature Reserve. There are also extensive areas of pavement in the Orton and Asby areas in east Cumbria. It is a tragedy that many pavements have been destroyed or damaged by the removal of surface rock for decorative use in the garden trade.

Anyone exploring a limestone pavement for the first time will be excited by this totally unique habitat. The pavements are often flat, bare expanses of limestone which were subjected to the erosive action of melting ice sheets after glaciation and since then rain water has dissolved the limestone and widened cracks to form deep fissures called 'grikes'. These grikes, which may be several feet deep, catch wind-blown soil and the run-off of water from the surrounding rock surface. They provide a sheltered and humid habitat which, furthermore, cannot be reached by grazing animals. The plants found here include Hart's Tongue Fern, Herb Robert, Dog's Mercury and such rare or uncommon species as Dark Red Helleborine, Angular Solomon's Seal, Lily of the Valley, Dropwort and Wall Lettuce. Most characteristic of limestone pavement are perhaps the ferns, which include in their number the rare Rigid Buckler, Limestone Polypody and Holly Fern.

▼ Limestone pavement forms a unique habitat where rare plants often thrive in the sheltered conditions of the rock fissures.

▼ The Wheatear, a summer visitor, derives its name from its 'white rear' which is especially conspicuous when the bird is in flight.

▲ The Rockrose is a common plant of limestone grassland. Its large yellow flowers may be seen between June and August.

▲ The Wood Tiger Moth occurs on grassland, heaths and moors. The male may sometimes be seen flying on warm, sunny days.

▲ Biting Stonecrop is most often seen growing on rocky areas, but also occurs on grassland, and sand and shingle along the coast. The leaves have a hot, peppery taste.

▲ The rare Lily of the Valley may occasionally be found growing on limestone pavement or in limestone woodland. It flowers in May and June, and later bears poisonous red berries.

▼ The strange-looking fern, Moonwort, can easily be overlooked as its green fronds blend so well with the grassland in which it grows.

▼ The rare Dark Red Helleborine occurs locally in the limestone pavements and woodlands of the region. It flowers between June and July.

Woodlands

Before man began to have a significant impact on the landscape, much of the land up to quite an altitude was covered by woodland. Now only fragments of this ancient woodland exist, but in these can be found more species of plants and animals than in any other habitat in the region. In more recent centuries new woodlands have been planted for amenity or profit, and in some areas they have regenerated naturally, to produce in total a wide range of woodland habitats.

▲ Juniper, an evergreen, occurs on limestone and upland acidic soils; it may grow, at high altitude, as the prostrate form shown here, or, at lower levels, as a tall upright shrub.

Limestone Woodland and Scrub

In limestone woodland and scrub, many of the plants found in other limestone areas occur, together with the more specialized woodland species. The characteristic tree is Ash, and Elm, Hazel, Silver Birch, Yew, Whitebeam, Rowan and Lime may also be present. Many shrubs also occur – Buckthorn, Blackthorn, Juniper, Guelder Rose, Hawthorn and Spindle being typical.

The ground flora is often rich and varied with a number of rare or local species including Lily of the Valley, Green and Stinking Hellebores, Columbine, Angular Soloman's Seal, Herb Paris and Spurge Laurel. Of the orchid family Broadleaved and Dark Red Helleborines, Early Purple, Butterfly, Birdsnest and Fly Orchids may be found. Deadly Nightshade with its large purple-black berries, grows in a number of the woods. This is quite a rare plant, not to be confused with Woody Nightshade whose berries are red. Other plants common on limestone but also found in other types of woodland include Bluebell, Primrose, Cowslip, Wild Daffodil, Wood Sorrel, Wood Anemone, Dog's Mercury, Lords and Ladies, Ground Ivy, Valerian, Wood Avens and Lesser Celandine.

▼ Coppicing is an old method of woodland management whereby trees, often Hazel, are periodically cut back to a stump. New shoots grow up from the stump which will later be suitable for broom handles, fencing and other uses. Plants such as Wood Anemone thrive in the open conditions after felling.

Lowland Mixed Woodlands

Many of the mixed woodlands in lowland areas grow on acid to neutral soils and are dominated by Oaks, with Birch, Rowan, Hazel and Holly. Wild Cherry, Crab Apple, and Hawthorn are often present, and in some woods Yew and Scots Pine, Larch and Beech may be common. These woods generally have a sparse shrub layer unless they were former coppice or coppice-with-standards woods. Hazel was most commonly coppiced while large Oak standards provided timber for building.

The ground flora on the more acid soils includes Bilberry, Wavy Hair and other grasses, Lady, Male and Broad Buckler Ferns and Bracken. In areas of richer soil where Ash and Wych Elm grow can be found Bramble, Sanicle, Dog's Mercury, Self Heal, Bugle and Wood Pimpernel.

Wet areas, beside small streams, often contain Alder and the shrubs Alder Buckthorn and Guelder Rose together with a different ground flora which includes tall herbs such as Touch-me-Not, Hemp Agrimony, Wild Angelica and Valerian. Alder is common along rivers and lake shores where with several species of Willow it may form 'carr', or wet woodland.

▲ Lords and Ladies, a plant of woodland and hedgerows, flowers between April and June.

▼ Guelder Rose has clusters of white flowers in summer, and later bears red berries.

▲ Lakeland is one of the few areas in Britain where our only native balsam, Touch-me-not, occurs. It grows in damp shady places and flowers between July and September.

▲ Herb Paris occurs locally in woods on limestone. It flowers between May and July, and usually has four leaves which form a whorl; the single flower later turns into a poisonous black berry.

▼ Rowan, one of the most beautiful trees tolerant of acid soils, occurs high on mountains and moorland as well as in lowland woods.

Upland Woodland

High on the valley sides of the Lake District the hanging Oakwoods represent remnants of ancient woodlands growing on ground too steep for timber exploitation, although many of the more accessible Oaks were often cut for coppice. Oak, Birch and Rowan may be the only common trees here, with Juniper growing higher up on rocky ground. Grazing sheep usually limit the variety of the ground flora and can also prevent tree regeneration, but there can be a rich moss and lichen flora on boulders and tree trunks.

Alder woodland is also found on wet valleysides and here a more diverse range of shrubs and herbs can be found, including Bird Cherry, with its small, bitter fruits.

Conifer Plantations

Much new woodland has been planted over the last century. This consists mainly of conifer plantations, which have been the target of a great deal of criticism, not only because the uniform blocks of trees are not very pleasing to the eye, but also because their wildlife can be very poor in comparison with other types of woodland. Conifer woodlands are essentially a commercial crop, but where there has been skilful planting to create a variety of tree species, ages and spacing, and where natural features such as crags, mires and clearings have not been obscured, attractive and interesting forests have been created. Such are the plantations on the west side of Thirlmere, and parts of Grizedale Forest where there are nature trails and deer-watching hides. In some plantations nest boxes are provided to encourage breeding birds such as tits.

▼ The Long-eared Owl, which has orange eyes, occurs mainly in coniferous woods. It often uses the old nests of other birds, such as Crows.

Woodland Fauna

Among the birds of fellside woodlands are Chaffinch, Robin, Blackbird, Coal Tit, and Wren. Several summer migrants such as the Wood Warbler, Willow Warbler, Pied Flycatcher, Redstart and Tree Pipit are also typical hill country species.

In woods at lower levels, Treecreeper and Green and Great Spotted Woodpeckers are widespread; Nuthatch occurs locally, and the elusive Hawfinch is not uncommon in parts of southern Lakeland. Where there is more undergrowth Chiffchaff, Garden Warbler and Blackcap are attracted. Other woodland birds include Bullfinch, Long-tailed Tit, Marsh Tit, Tawny Owl, Jay, Magpie, Spotted Flycatcher and Woodcock.

Carrion Crow, Sparrowhawk and Buzzard nest in both woodland and forest, whilst a number of birds, such as the seed eating Crossbill and Siskin, have actually benefited from conifer planting. Young plantations which harbour small mammals such as voles, provide good hunting for Kestrels and Owls.

▲ The Blackcap, a summer visitor, nests in woodland scrub. The male (shown here) helps incubate the eggs and feed the young.

▼ The Woodcock blends well with the dead twigs and leave's it nests amongst; if disturbed it has been known to carry its young to safety.

Roe Deer are typical mammals of the woodlands, though it is often only their tracks which are seen. The main strongholds of the Red Deer are in Martindale Forest (a mostly tree-less area) and the Furness Fells where they feed for preference either in the open, or on grassy woodland floors, and, in autumn, on acorns in Oakwoods. Red Squirrels are common and are frequently seen in the woods of Furness and Borrowdale. Foxes and Badgers are also common, although Badgers occur more locally. Voles and Wood Mice, Stoats, Weasels and Shrews are widespread in woodland.

In spring, the Orange Tip butterfly is common along woodland margins and in clearings. In the south of the region, including southern Lakeland, many butterflies may be seen including Brimstone, Brown Argus, both Purple and Green Hairstreak, Dingy Skipper, Duke of Burgundy and Dark Green Fritillary. The common Green Tortrix Moth occurs in Oakwoods, its larvae sometimes almost completely stripping the leaves from trees.

▼ The Redstart, a summer visitor, nests in holes in trees or stone walls. It is most likely to be noticed by the flash of its red tail as it disappears into cover. The female is duller in colour and lacks the black and white head markings of the male.

▲ The Dark Green Fritillary is a large fast-flying butterfly of the more open woodland areas; it is on the wing in July and August.

▲ The Crossbill occurs in some conifer plantations; its specially adapted beak enables it to extract seeds from pine and other cones.

▲ The Hawfinch is not uncommon in the woods of southern Lakeland. It has an extremely powerful bill with which it can crack hard fruit stones.

▼ Now rare in most parts of England, the Red Squirrel has one of its strongholds in the woodlands of the Lake District.

Lakes, Rivers and Wetlands

Lakes and Tarns

Although Cumbria has more large areas of open water than any other region in England, many of the lakes and tarns of central Lakeland are deep, stony-shored or steep-sided, and therefore relatively poor in plant and bird life. In the lower lying areas the lakes with well-vegetated margins and the shallower reedy pools support a greater variety of wildlife.

Among the birds which breed around the open waters are the Mute Swan, Mallard, Teal and Tufted Duck, and on some lakes, the introduced Greylag and Canada Geese. The Red-breasted Merganser has spread inland from the coast, and the Goosander has recently extended its range southward into Cumbria. Great Crested and Little Grebes breed on some quieter waters, and, on undisturbed shingle shores, Common Sandpiper may nest. Herons are often seen fishing along the lake shores, rivers and becks (streams), possibly several miles away from their tree-top nests. Moorhen and Coot are common breeding birds, the latter often being seen in flocks of several hundreds in winter.

Other birds seen in winter include Cormorant, Goldeneye, Pochard and Whooper Swan, with the largest numbers being found on the shallow reaches of the larger lakes. Occasionally visitors such as Smew, Common and Velvet Scoters, Black-throated and Great Northern Divers are seen. Gull roosts are conspicuous features of some lakes especially in winter with Common, Black-headed, Herring and Greater Black-backed Gulls usually present. A number of man-made water bodies including lowland reservoirs and flooded pits, can also be rich in bird life, and if good marginal vegetation has developed some interesting breeding birds may occur.

The plants to look for in shallow water include Water Lobelia, Yellow and White Water Lilies, Quillwort, various pondweeds, Water Starwort, Shoreweed and Awlwort.

▼ Rydal Water, near Ambleside, one of the more nutrient-rich waters in the region. Common Reed and other marginal vegetation can be seen growing along its sheltered shoreline.

Near or around the edge of many waters there are sometimes areas of wetland. Where these water bodies are poor in plant nutrients the wetland will usually have a poor flora, perhaps containing sedges, rushes, *Sphagnum* mosses, Purple Moor Grass, Heath Spotted Orchid and other plants typical of more acidic conditions.

A more luxuriant type of wetland, commonly known as fen, develops on the shores of richer waters. The most conspicuous plant here is Common Reed; Reed-grass, Yellow Iris, Reedmace, Yellow Loosestrife, and smaller plants such as Water Plantain, Water Mint and Forget-me-Nots may also occur. Willows and Alder often grow in these fens.

These still water margins, and other sluggish waters, are amongst the best places to see those spectacular insects, dragonflies and damselflies. The large Golden-ringed Dragonfly with its black and yellow abdomen is very distinctive; common damselflies include the Large Red, Common Blue and the Common Ischnura.

▲ The Golden-ringed Dragonfly may be seen resting on vegetation, often well away from water.

▲ The unmistakeable flowers of the White Water-lily may be seen during July and August.

▲ The introduced Canada Goose is now established in Britain as a breeding bird and occurs on many of the region's waters.

▲ Globeflower is a sub-alpine meadow species which grows locally in damp grassland and along streams and lakes. It flowers between June and August.

▼ Whooper Swans, so named for their bugle-like whooping calls, may be seen in winter on lakes and wet meadows of the region. In spring they return to their northern breeding grounds.

▼ The Great Crested Grebe occurs on a number of waters and in spring its spectacular mating displays may be seen. It builds a raft of floating vegetation for its nest.

Rivers and Becks

Many of the rivers and becks of the region are swift-flowing, allowing little growth of vegetation. A few species such as Watercress and Water Crowfoot manage to survive where a little shelter occurs. On undisturbed banks, Figwort, Skullcap, Water Dropwort, Globeflower, Great Burnet and Marsh Marigold can be found, often with many other species, especially where a damp meadow adjoins the water. The introduced Policeman's Helmet and Monkey Flower continue to spread and add colour to becksides and lake shores.

The birds to be found include the beautiful Kingfisher, which is most often seen on lower reaches where suitable steep banks can be found for its nest. Dippers breed on the middle to upper reaches, and Pied and Grey Wagtails and various ducks may also be common. Many woodland birds breed in riverside woodlands and several species may be seen coming to drink. Pied Flycatchers, for instance, often show a preference for suitable woodland sites near water. Mammals found alongside running water include Water Vole, Water Shrew, and more rarely Otter and Mink.

▲ The Kingfisher is most often seen as a blue flash as it flies swiftly along a river or lake shore.

▼ The Dipper frequents high, fast-flowing waters; it is able to both walk and swim under water.

Raised Mire and Flood Plains

A number of wetlands have already been mentioned. There are two further types which are of great interest to the naturalist and of which there are good examples in this region.

On the coastal plains around Morecambe Bay and the Solway Firth are extensive raised mires, known locally as mosses. These are flat or slightly domed areas of deep peat on which grow a range of acid-loving plants including Cotton Grass, Ling, Cross-leaved Heath, Cranberry, Bog Rosemary, Bog Myrtle, Bog Pimpernel, Bog Asphodel, Sundews, sedges and *Sphagnum* mosses. These boggy mires are especially rich in insects; the Large Heath Butterfly, many species of rare moths and the rare White Faced Dragonfly are some which may be seen in this habitat.

A final type of wetland occurs on large flood plains, the most interesting example being Leighton Moss in North Lancashire which is a reserve of the Royal Society for the Protection of Birds. Here water drains off limestone and is rich in plant nutrients, so supporting a fen type vegetation with

▼ The Grey Wagtail haunts swift-flowing waters; it nests in a niche in a rock face, or in a stone wall.

extensive reed beds and Willow scrub. There are also areas of open water, some the result of flooding old peat cuttings. Some of the vigorous reed growth around the pools is controlled by herbicide spraying and by cutting, to give more edge and mud areas for waders and dabbling ducks; this also enables other plants to colonize the area (see page 25).

The reserve is rich in bird life, with Bittern, Water Rail, Bearded Reedling, Sedge Warbler and Reed Warbler, which is rare this far north, all associated with the reed beds. Ducks include Pintail, Pochard, Shoveler and Garganey. The reserve is also visited by a variety of waders including Green, Common and Wood Sandpipers, Little Stint and Greenshank.

Canals

Old canals can be rewarding places to study wildlife. The Lancaster–Kendal canal, for example, contains some navigable stretches and other unused sections, and has a good variety of wildlife. A Canal Bank Nature Trail has been set up over a section near Stainton (see page 101). Common waterway plants including Reed-grass, Marsh Woundwort, Water Mint, Wild Angelica and Water Plantain can be seen here, together with aquatic species such as Branched Bur-reed, pondweeds and Spiked Water-milfoil and stagnant water species such as the Duckweeds. Many invertebrates also favour this habitat and provide food for some of the birds and larger insects seen by the canal.

▲ Bog Myrtle in flower. This aromatic shrub grows in acid bogs and on wet heaths. Each plant bears either orange (male) or red (female) catkins.

▲ The Large Heath Butterfly inhabits boggy areas in northern Britain where its food plant, the White Beak-sedge grows.

▼ The Bittern and Water Rail find cover in the extensive reed beds of Leighton Moss. The Otter also occurs on the reserve.

The Coast

The coasts of Cumbria and North Lancashire are amongst the most interesting in Britain for the naturalist. There are many types of habitat ranging from mudflats and saltmarshes of estuaries, to extensive shingle beaches and sand dunes. Sandstone cliffs occur around St Bees Head, this being an important breeding site for sea birds such as Puffin, Fulmar, Kittiwake, Cormorant, Guillemot, Razorbill and the rare Black Guillemot. Limestone cliffs are found at the head of Morecambe Bay, and these hold some interesting limestone and maritime plants.

Mudflats and Saltmarshes

The tidal mudflats and saltmarshes of the Ribble Estuary, Morecambe Bay and Solway Firth hold some of Europe's largest concentrations of wading birds. The best place to see these is the intertidal zone, where at various times of the year huge flocks of Knot, Sanderling, Redshank, Dunlin and Oystercatcher may be found. There are also large flocks of Grey and Ringed Plovers, Curlew, Bar-tailed Godwit and Turnstone. Other waders seen regularly on passage include Whimbrel, Greenshank, and Spotted Redshank. Occasionally rarities are found, such as one of the Phalaropes or a Pectoral Sandpiper. Mallard is one of the ducks most commonly seen on the intertidal area; others include Shelduck, which feeds mainly on small molluscs, and Wigeon, which feeds on Eel-grass.

In the deeper water Goldeneye, Scaup and Common Scoter occur, and occasionally the rarer Long-tailed Duck may be seen. Other sea ducks include Red-breasted Merganser and Eider.

In more sheltered bays, or wherever mud builds up, saltmarsh plants begin to colonize. Species such as Glasswort and Cord Grasses are first to establish, and these gather more mud and silt allowing further development of the saltmarsh. Plants to look for include Sea Arrowgrass, Common Sea Lavender, Sea Sandwort, Sea Aster and Sea Purslane. Many ducks and geese feed on saltmarshes; these include Wigeon, Pintail, Teal, Shoveler and Mallard. Of the geese, Pink-footed, White-fronted and Barnacle are regular winter visitors on parts of the coast while Greylag may be seen at any time.

▼ The tidal mudflats of Morecambe Bay support large populations of wading birds.

▼ The Greylag Goose, ancestor of our domestic geese, grazes on short turf.

▼ The Pink-footed Goose, a winter visitor, sometimes occurs in large numbers along the coast.

Shingle and Sand dunes

The shingle beaches around Walney Island and Sandscale are the second most extensive in the country and have a very rich flora. Plants establishing themselves above the reach of storm waves include the Yellow Horned Poppy, Sea Rocket, Sea Campion, Biting Stonecrop, Isle of Man Cabbage, Sea Beet, Sea Kale and very occasionally the rare Oyster Plant.

Behind the shingle areas, windblown sand often accumulates as dunes, which are colonized by pioneering plants such as Marram Grass and Sea Couch-grass. These help stabilize the dunes and also trap more sand, so the dunes increase in size. Other plants such as Sea Bindweed, Prickly Saltwort and Sea Holly may be found on the younger dunes whilst in the dry hollows amongst older, more stable dunes a wide variety of plants may grow. These include Creeping Willow, Bird's Foot Trefoil, Rest-harrow, Kidney Vetch, Wild Thyme, Sea Spurge, Whitlow-grass, Carline Thistle, Seaside Centaury, Round-leaved Wintergreen and Dune Pansy. Many dune systems also contain wet hollows or slacks, some of which hold brackish water from sea flooding. Others contain freshwater and hold species such as Marsh Pennywort, Grass of Parnassus, Dune and Marsh Helleborines, and various other marsh orchids. Some of the slacks are home for the nationally rare Natterjack Toad.

▲ Grass of Parnassus grows in coastal dune slacks and wet flushes inland. Its delicate flowers may be seen between June and September.

▲ The rare Natterjack Toad still survives in a number of sand dune areas along the coast.

▼ The Little and Sandwich Terns nest on shingle beaches. Yellow Horned Poppy is in flower between June and September.

Five species of tern are to be found breeding on the shingle and dune areas in the region; these are the Common Tern, Arctic Tern, Sandwich Tern, Little Tern and the rare Roseate Tern. There are also some very large gull colonies. Shelduck nest in some of the dunes, and on Walney Island the Eider Duck also breeds. Other birds nesting on sand and shingle include Oystercatcher and Ringed Plover.

The coast also provides migration watch points, such as Grune Point and South Walney Nature Reserve, where various warblers, chats and many other species can be seen in spring and autumn. Occasionally rare migrants such as Hoopoe, Wryneck and Icterine Warbler may also be seen at these times.

Seabirds such as Gannet and Skuas may be seen flying past, especially when strong winds force the birds closer inshore. There is also good fishing off the coast for Bass, Dab, Plaice, Whiting and Cod. Bottle-nosed Dolphins and both Common and Grey Seals are seen infrequently, and on rare occasions Basking Shark may be sighted.

▼ The rare Seaside Centaury occurs locally on sand dunes in the region. It flowers in July and August and has rather leathery leaves.

▲ The Shelduck may be seen on sandy or muddy shores of saltmarshes and estuaries.

▲ Cumbria is the most southerly part of Britain where the Eider Duck breeds. Its down has long been used as an insulating material.

▼ The Razorbill spends most of its time well out at sea, it breeds on cliff faces and, at this time, may be seen in the area of St Bees Head.

▼ The Kittiwake, our only true maritime gull, usually only ventures ashore to breed.

Farmland

The richness of wildlife on farmland and therefore its attraction to the naturalist, varies considerably throughout the region. In the poorest examples, agricultural improvements in the form of land drainage, heavy use of fertilizers and chemical sprays, the uprooting of hedgerows and earlier hay cutting have made it impossible for many species of plants and animals to survive. The Corncrake and Quail are two species which have declined so rapidly that in future few people will ever hear their evocative calls.

In the good areas however a wide variety of wildlife can be found on farmland, especially in copses, shelter belts, hedges, rough grassland, wet meadows, ponds and even around the buildings themselves. Skylark, Meadow Pipit and Partridge inhabit open fields, in which damper areas attract birds such as Lapwing, Snipe, Redshank and Curlew. Cuckoos are also found here, the main hosts for their eggs in this habitat being Meadow Pipit, Skylark and Yellow Wagtail.

Hedges and rough corners with scrub may have Chaffinch, Yellowhammer, Goldfinch, Linnet, Dunnock, Whitethroat and occasionally Corn Bunting or Whinchat. Old trees and copses may also attract larger birds such as Rook, Carrion Crow, Jackdaw, Magpie, Mistle Thrush, Tawny Owl and Little Owl.

Other birds use the farmland as feeding areas. Black-headed Gulls are found at any time of year, often joined by large numbers of Common Gulls in winter. Blackbirds and Song Thrushes also feed here together in winter with Redwings and Fieldfares. Other winter visitors include Brambling and on higher farms, especially where sheep are being fed hay or other plants with seeds, Snow Buntings are occasionally found. Very rarely Waxwings visit hedges or gardens to feed on berries, and among the birds found around farmyards and buildings are Kestrel, Barn Owl, House Sparrow, Robin, Pied Wagtail, House Martin, Swift and Swallow.

Of the mammals found on farmland, the House Mouse, Wood Mouse, Bank Vole, Field Vole and Rabbit are often common and provide prey for Stoats and Weasels. The Fox is frequent and the Badger local. Various species of deer come onto farmland to feed and bats such as Long-eared, Pipistrelle and Daubenton's sometimes roost in trees or buildings.

▼ Lakeland meadow with Melancholy Thistle and Meadowsweet blooming in the uncut edge.

▲ The Curlew nests mainly in damp meadows and moors. In winter it is common along the coast.

▼ The Redshank builds its nest amongst tall vegetation in damp meadows, moors and marshes.

Plants

Some of the plants found in farmland are well-known weeds such as Nettle, Docks and Thistles, but with the use of herbicides some attractive weeds such as Poppies, Field Pansy, Large-flowered Hemp Nettle, and Corn Cockle are declining and, in some areas, are even extinct.

The most interesting collections of plants are found in the traditional hay meadows and permanent pastures, which have escaped 'improvement'. In the richest of these, over one hundred different species of flowering plants may be found. Typical northern meadow plants include Wood Cranesbill, Great Burnet, Melancholy Thistle, Lady's Mantle, Water Avens and Globeflower. Rich flushes, especially in upland pastures, may contain Birdseye Primrose, Grass of Parnassus, Saw-wort, Twayblade and Fragrant Orchid. Other orchids found in meadows include Northern Marsh, Heath and Common Spotted, Small White, Frog, Greater and Lesser Butterfly Orchids.

Hayfields should not be entered to observe these plants at close quarters since this is the farmer's crop. However many of Cumbria's roadside verges are well worth studying for their large numbers of species, including most of the plants named above. The limestone areas around Arnside, Silverdale, Shap, Alston and Greystoke are particularly rewarding, especially where wide verges occur.

▲ The Barn Owl hunts by night over farmland and open woodland; its diet consists mainly of small rodents. Over past years its numbers have declined, partly due to use of pesticides.

▲ Wood Cranesbill, a plant uncommon south of Cumbria, may be seen in hay meadows, hedgebanks and in the mountains of the region.

▼ Northern Marsh Orchid (left) flowers in marshes, fens and damp pastures between June and July, occasionally its leaves are spotted. Twayblade (centre), another member of the orchid family, occurs in meadows and woods, flowering between May and July. Melancholy Thistle (right) is locally common in upland meadows; it is not prickly, and its large serrated leaves are white on the underside.

Common Species of the Countryside and Seashore

Some of Britain's animals and plants can be found only in certain regions, or are more easily found in some areas than in others. Living alongside these rare or local species are, of course, many animals and plants which are fairly widespread throughout the country. The more common species of British birds, wild flowers, trees, butterflies, mammals and seashore animals are illustrated on the following pages. These illustrations form a basic field guide to the majority of the regions in Britain.

The captions to the bird illustrations indicate the bird's usual haunts, and if it is seen only in certain seasons, this fact is mentioned. Measurements indicate the size of the bird from the tip of the beak to the end of the tail. Notes to aid identification of the species are also included.

The mammals that are illustrated are accompanied by captions which indicate their average size. Those for hoofed mammals indicate their height at the shoulder. Others indicate the length of their bodies from nose to rump. The captions also give an indication as to when the animal is most active and therefore most easily observed.

The wild flowers are grouped according to their commonest colours; their most frequently used names are given in the captions, along with their habitats, the months in which they flower and their height or the length of creeping stems if they grow horizontally.

The illustrations of butterflies frequently show them on the plants they prefer to visit. The captions indicate the butterflies' usual habitats, the months when they are most frequently seen, and their wingspan.

Information about the sizes of the seashore animals are detailed in their captions, while the height of the trees is given on page 96. Selected identifying characteristics are given in the captions to the trees.

A hedgerow in early summer—one of the countryside's most rewarding habitats, since it shelters a wide variety of species. This illustration features some of the common, widespread plants and animals included in the following pages.

Birds

Canada Goose ▶

Fields and marshes near water; parks. Brown wings and body. Introduced from Canada. 95 cm.

Shag ▶

Rocky coats, where it nests in colonies. Has crest only in breeding season. Flies low, close to the water. 78 cm.

Cormorant ▶

Near the sea and some large inland waters. Has white thigh patch in breeding season. Larger than Shag. 92 cm.

Spring

◀ Mute Swan

Wide rivers, lakes, town parks. Not, as its name implies, mute. Britain's most common swan. 152 cm.

▼ Wigeon
Near sea, especially in winter; lakes and marshes. Seen August-April; a few stay to breed. 46 cm.

Mallard ▲
Inland waters and estuaries. Purplish-blue wing patch seen in flight. 58 cm.

◀ Pintail
Lakes and marshes, near coast in winter. Pointed tail and long, elegant neck. Seen September-March; a few stay to breed. 66 cm.

Shoveler ▶
Quiet lakes and shallow water. Large, heavy bill. Pale blue forewings of both male and female show in flight. 51 cm.

▼ Teal
Inland waters and estuaries. The smallest duck in Britain. Dark bill. Quick and agile in flight. 35 cm.

▲ Tufted Duck
Lakes, ponds, gravel pits and parks. Dumpy, active diving duck. Note female's yellow eye. 43 cm.

▲ Shelduck

Coasts and estuaries, often in flocks; also large inland lakes. Female has no red knob on bill. 61 cm.

▼ Pochard

Lakes and backwaters. In flight, both sexes have dark wings with paler grey central bar. 46 cm.

▲ Red-breasted Merganser

Coastal areas; wooded lakes, rivers, in breeding season. 58 cm.

Grey Heron ▶

Near water: rivers, lakes and seashores. Head is drawn back in flight. 92 cm.

▲ Great Crested Grebe

Inland waters, sometimes on sea in winter. 48 cm.

▼ Little Grebe

Inland waters. Secretive and hard to spot. 27 cm.

Buzzard ▼

Often seen soaring over moors and farmland. Rare in east and south-east England. 54 cm.

▼ Kestrel

Moors, coasts, farmland; some nest in towns. Hovers when hunting. 34 cm.

Coot ►

Lakes, reservoirs, open water. Larger, heavier bird than Moorhen. 38 cm.

▲ Moorhen

Ponds, lakes and streams. 33 cm.

◄ Partridge

Farmland, moors. Small head, short tail and legs. Often in small groups. 30 cm.

♂

▼ Pheasant

Farmland, scrub, woodland. Males can have white neckring. Male 87 cm, female 58 cm.

♀

◄ **Redshank**
Seashores and wet meadows. Probes in mud. 28 cm.

▼ **Oystercatcher**
Seashores, estuaries. Often in groups. White band on throat in winter. 43 cm.

▲ **Turnstone**
Shingle or rocky coasts. Turns over stones, seaweed, to find food. 23 cm.

Common Sandpiper ▲
Rivers, streams and lakes. Seen April-October; a few in winter. 20 cm.

▼ **Ringed Plover**
Sandy and muddy shores. In summer, white wing bar shows in flight. 19 cm.

Lapwing ▲
Farmland, marshes, mudflats. 30 cm.

Curlew ▶
Mudflats and estuaries in winter; farmland, moors in breeding season. Rare in East Anglia and the South-East as a breeder. Britain's largest wader. 48-64 cm.

Winter

▲ Bar-tailed Godwit
Coastal mudflats and estuaries. Smaller than Black-tailed Godwit. 37 cm.

Winter

Black-tailed Godwit ▶
Coasts in winter; inland lakes, marshes in breeding season. White wing bar in summer. 41 cm.

◀ Whimbrel
Coastal mudflats and estuaries; meadows near the sea. 40 cm.

Woodcock ▼
Damp woods; not seen on shore. Secretive. 34 cm.

▲ Dunlin

Mudflats and estuaries. Common winter shorebird; less common in summer. 19 cm.

▲ Sanderling

Sandy shores along coasts. Seen August-May. Short, straight beak. 20 cm.

◀ Ruff

Marshes, wet meadows, edges of reservoirs. Seen mostly in spring and autumn. 29 cm.

Snipe ▼

Wet fields, marshes or lake edges. Probes while standing still. 27 cm.

Greenshank ▼

Coasts, marshes. Seen chiefly on migration. Some breed in Scotland. 30 cm.

▼ Knot

Sand or mudflats in estuaries. Larger than Dunlin. Seen mostly August-May. 25 cm.

▼ Common Tern

Near sea; also nests inland in Scotland. Seen April-October. 34 cm.

Summer

◀ Little Tern

Shingle beaches. Never has full black cap like other terns. Seen April-September. 24 cm.

Summer

Herring Gull ▼

Coastal ports and seaside towns. Wingtips are black with white spots. 56 cm.

Summer

◀ Black-headed Gull

Inland and near the sea. Dark brown "hood" in summer only. 37 cm.

Summer

Common Gull ▶

Coasts; often inland in winter. Smaller and less widespread than Herring Gull. 41 cm.

Lesser Black-backed Gull ▶

Coasts and inland. Mainly a summer visitor. 53 cm.

▼ Guillemot

Rocky coasts. Neck and throat are white in winter. Seen at cliff sites December-August. 42 cm.

◀ Fulmar

Rocky coasts. Nests on cliffs. Always sits, never stands. Mostly out at sea in winter. 47 cm.

Puffin ▶

Rocky islands and sea cliffs. Colourful bill in summer. 30 cm.

▼ Collared Dove

Large gardens, parks and farmland. Long white tail with black base. 30 cm.

◀ Stock Dove

Woods and cliffs; sometimes in towns. Darker, smaller bird than Woodpigeon. 33 cm.

Rock Dove ▼

Coasts, usually on sea cliffs. Town pigeons are descended from these birds. 33 cm.

Woodpigeon ▶

Farmland, woods and towns. White neck patch on adult. 41 cm.

▼ Short-eared Owl
Open country. Hunts in day-time or at dusk. 37 cm.

◀ Barn Owl
Open country, especially farmland. Mostly nocturnal. 34 cm.

Little Owl ▼
Farmland and wooded country. Underside is streaked. Often seen in daylight. 22 cm.

◀ Long-eared Owl
Edges of woods. Underside all dark. Nocturnal. 34 cm.

▲ Tawny Owl
Parks, woodland and farmland; sometimes towns. Large head. Nocturnal. 38 cm.

▼ Cuckoo
Anywhere in countryside. Male's song is well known. April-September. 30 cm.

◀ Kingfisher
Near rivers and lakes; seashore in winter. Dives from low perch or from a hover. 17 cm.

Swift ▶
Breeds mainly in towns; may fly over countryside. Seen end of April-August/September. 17 cm.

▼ Sand Martin
Banks and sandy cliffs. Seen April-September. 12 cm.

◀ House Martin
Suburban areas and countryside. Seen April-October. 13 cm.

◀ Swallow
Farms and open country; often near water. Seen April-September/October. 19 cm.

◀ Great Spotted Woodpecker
Woodlands. Large white patches on wings. 23 cm.

◀ Green Woodpecker
Deciduous woods, parks. Yellow-green rump seen in flight. Rare in Scotland. 32 cm.

Lesser Spotted Woodpecker ▶
Deciduous woods, parks. Not in Scotland. Sparrow-sized. 14 cm.

▼ Dunnock

Bushes and shrubs everywhere. Slender bill, unlike sparrows. 14.5 cm.

▲ Meadow Pipit

Upland moors and other open areas. Smaller, daintier than larks. 14.5 cm.

Tree Pipit ▲

Heaths and areas with scattered trees. Seen April-September. 15 cm.

▲ Skylark

Open country, especially farmland. Rises vertically to a great height in song flight. 18 cm.

♂

◀ Yellow Wagtail

Grassy places near water. Seen April-late September. 17 cm.

♂

Summer

◀ Grey Wagtail

By lochs or fast-flowing hill steams; waterfalls in lowlands. 18 cm.

▲ Pied Wagtail

Towns and countryside, usually near water. Females are greyer. Takes insects from the ground or the air. 18 cm.

▼ Willow Warbler
Gardens, woods and hedgerows. Flatter head and longer tail than Chiffchaff. Seen April-September. 11 cm.

▲ Sedge Warbler
Thick vegetation near water. Broad, pale stripe over eye. Seen April-September. 13 cm.

Wren ►
Towns and countryside. Tiny, rotund bird with cocked tail. 9.5 cm.

Reed Warbler ▼
Reed beds. Not in Scotland. Seen April-September. 13 cm.

▲ Blackcap
Wooded areas. Seen April-September, a few in winter. 14 cm.

▼ Whitethroat
Thick, low bushes. Seen April-September. 14 cm.

▲ Garden Warbler
Hedges or woods with thick undergrowth. Seen April-September. 14 cm.

Chiffchaff ▼
Woods and copses. Seen March-September; a few in winter. 11 cm.

▲ Wood Warbler
Open woods with sparse undergrowth. Seen April-August. 13 cm.

Wheatear ▼
Open country, especially moors and downs. Seen March-October. 15 cm.

▲ Whinchat
Rough grassland, moors with scrub, bracken, etc. Seen April-September. 13 cm.

◀ Pied Flycatcher
Deciduous woods, especially oak. Seen April-September. 13 cm.

Spotted Flycatcher ▶
Parks, gardens, open woods. Seen May-September. 14 cm.

Blackbird ▼

In trees and bushes everywhere. Young are paler than female with breast more strongly spotted. 25 cm.

▼ Starling

Most places, including cities. In summer, has purple and green gloss and mostly yellow bill. 22 cm.

▲ Redwing

Farmland, commons and other open areas. A few breed in Scotland. Seen October-April. 21 cm.

◀ Fieldfare

Farmland, orchards, open areas. White underwings. Seen October-April. 25.5 cm.

▼ Redstart

Heaths, parks, open woods. Seen April-September. Rather Robin-like. 14 cm.

Robin ▲

Gardens, hedgerows and woodland. Juvenile is spotted, without any red. 14 cm.

◀ Song Thrush
Trees and bushes in towns and country. Smashes snails on stones. 23 cm.

Long-tailed Tit ▶
Hedgerows and woodland edges. 14 cm. (7.5 cm of which is the tail).

◀ Great Tit
Gardens and woodlands. Black band on chest. 14 cm.

◀ Blue Tit
Woods and gardens. Dark line on belly. 11 cm.

▲ Mistle Thrush
Woodland and open areas. Larger than Blackbird; paler, greyer than Song Thrush. 27 cm.

▼ Marsh Tit
Deciduous woods; infrequently in gardens. 11 cm.

▲ Coal Tit
Coniferous woods, parks, gardens. Oblong white patch on nape. 11 cm.

▲ Siskin

Usually coniferous woods in summer; birch, alder woods, sometimes gardens, in winter. 11 cm.

▼ Chaffinch

Farmland, hedgerows and woodland. Male is duller in winter. White wing bar seen in flight. 15 cm.

▲ Nuthatch

Deciduous wood and parks. Can descend trees head-first. Very short tail. Rare in Scotland. 14 cm.

▲ Hawfinch

Deciduous woodland, orchards. Very elusive. Big head and massive, broad bill. 16 cm.

◀ Treecreeper

Woodland, sometimes parks and gardens. Creeps up tree trunks using tail as support. 13 cm.

▲ Goldfinch
Open country, orchards and gardens. Distinctive broad yellow band across black wing. 12 cm.

▲ Bullfinch
Deciduous woodlands, hedges, orchards, gardens. Whitish wing bar on black wing. 15 cm.

◀ Linnet
Heathland and farmland. Forms large flocks in autumn on fields and waste ground. 13 cm.

▼ Lesser Redpoll
Coniferous and birch woods. Male has pink breast in spring. Streaked flanks (unlike Linnet). 12 cm.

▲ Greenfinch
Hedgerows, parks and gardens. Forages in flocks from autumn to spring. 15 cm.

▲ House Sparrow
Near houses in cities; on farms in the country. Distinctive black bib on male. 15 cm.

▼ Tree Sparrow
Farmland. White cheeks with black spot. Sometimes flocks with House Sparrow in winter. 14 cm.

▲ Corn Bunting
Open country, especially cornfields. Bigger than other buntings and finches. 18 cm.

▲ Yellowhammer
Farmland, heaths, young plantations. Flocks forage in fields in winter. Rare in Wales. 17 cm.

▲ Goldcrest
Large gardens and woods, especially conifers. Smallest British bird. 9 cm.

▲ Reed Bunting
Vegetation near water; may visit bird tables in winter. Male has less black on head in winter. 15 cm.

Carrion Crow ▶

Open country, town, along coasts. Usually seen alone, in pairs or small groups. 47 cm.

▼ Jay

Woodlands, parks and gardens. White rump and blue wing flash show in flight. 32 cm.

◀ Magpie

Hedgerows, farmland, scrub. Large black and white bird. Long, slender tail. 46 cm.

▼ Jackdaw

Cliffs, farmland and towns. Small black and grey crow. Forms large flocks. 33 cm.

▲ Rook

Farmland, open copses, villages. Forms large flocks. Baggy thighs. Bare whitish face in adults. 46 cm.

Mammals

▼ Red Fox

Farmland and woods, sometimes mountains and towns. Mainly nocturnal. 65 cm.

▼ Roe Deer

Conifer plantations, especially near water. Mainly nocturnal; hides during day. 70 cm.

▲ Badger

Woods, sometimes mountains. Nocturnal. Can stay underground for several days in cold weather without food. 80 cm.

▲ Hedgehog

Hedgerows, ditches, parks, gardens and moorland. Mainly nocturnal. 25 cm.

▲ Mole

Underground in most kinds of soil in farmland, woods. Lives alone. Can swim well. 13 cm.

▼ Grey Squirrel
Woods, parks and gardens. Introduced from N. America. Diurnal. 27 cm.

Red Squirrel ▲
Mainly conifer woods. Partly replaced by Grey Squirrel in England. 23 cm.

▼ Rabbit
Farmland, woodland, sand dunes and hillsides. Active at dusk and dawn. 40 cm.

◄ Brown Hare
Open farmland and woodland. Mainly nocturnal, but can often be seen in day. 58 cm.

▼ Wood Mouse
Gardens, hedgerows, woods. Mainly nocturnal. 9 cm.

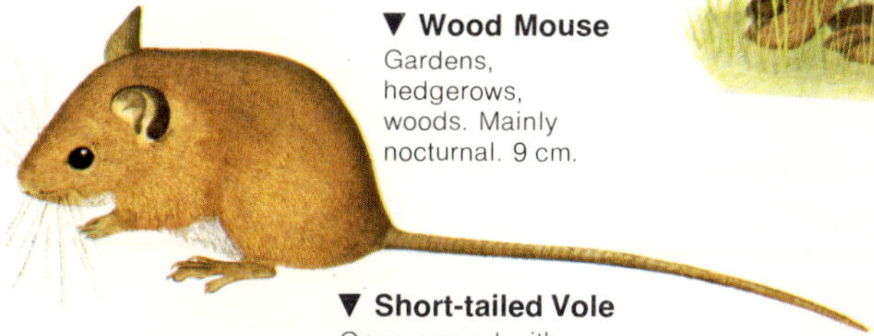

▼ Common Shrew
Rough pasture, woods, hedgerows, dunes and marshes. Active day and night. 7 cm.

▼ Short-tailed Vole
Open ground with rough grass. Most active at night; also seen in day. 11 cm.

◀ Grey Seal

Rocky shores, mainly along Atlantic coast; some on east coast of Scotland and north-east coast of England. 3 m.

Common Seal ▶

Flat shores, estuaries and mudbanks on Scottish coasts and mainly east coast of England. Blunter head than Grey Seal. 1.5 m.

◀ Stoat

Woods, farmland, mountains. Tip of tail always black. Mainly nocturnal. 28 cm.

▲ Weasel

Same habitat as Stoat, but prefers dry places. Mainly nocturnal. 20 cm.

Water Vole ▶

Ponds, canals, streams and marshes. Mainly diurnal. May also be black. 19 cm.

Otter ▶

Alongside rivers, lakes; marshes, coasts and the sea. Nocturnal. More common in Scotland. 70 cm.

Wild Flowers

▲ Lesser Celandine
Damp, shady woods, grassy banks and waysides. Creeping stems. March-May. 5-25 cm.

▼ Common St John's Wort
Damp, grassy places, open woods, hedgebanks. Less common in some northern areas. June-September. 30-90 cm.

◄ Bulbous Buttercup
Dry, grassy places. Base of stem is swollen and bulb-like. March-June. 15-40 cm.

▼ Creeping Buttercup
Damp grassy places, woods, gardens. Long, leafy, creeping runners. May-August. Runners 15-60 cm.

▼ Cowslip
Meadows, pastures, woods, copses. Absent from much of Scotland. April-May. 10-30 cm.

▼ Creeping Jenny
Grassy, shady places; damp meadows, woods, under hedges. Rare in northern Scotland. June-August. Stems up to 60 cm.

◀ Yellow Rattle
Waysides and other grassy places. Seeds rattle inside ripe capsule. May-August. 12-40 cm.

Common Rockrose ▶
Grassy, rocky places. Not a rose. Leaves are hairy.
May-September 5-30 cm.

Aaron's Rod ▶
Banks, waste places, open scrub. Rarer in Scotland. June-August. 30-200 cm.

◀ Groundsel
Waste places; a common garden weed. Flowers all year round. 8-45 cm.

▲ Primrose
Woods, hedges and fields. Rarer in the North. February-May. 8-15 cm.

◀ Herb Bennet
Woods, hedges, shady places. Fruits are hooked. June-August. 20-60 cm.

◀ Broom
Heaths, waste ground, open woods, scrubland. May-June. 60-200 cm.

▲ Yellow Pimpernel
Woods and shady hedgebanks. May-September. Trailing stems up to 40 cm long.

◀ Silverweed
Hedgebanks, grassy places. Creeping stems. May-August.

▲ Old Man's Beard
Woodland edges, hedgerows, scrub. Rare in Scotland and northern England. July-August. Up to 30 m.

Golden Rod ▶
Woods, cliffs, hedges. Rarer in the South-East. July-September. 5-75 cm.

▼ Bird's Foot Trefoil
Open, grassy places. Very long, creeping stems. Pods look like a bird's foot. May-June.

▼ Creeping Cinquefoil
Hedgebanks, grassy places. Creeping stems. May-August.

▲ Dandelion
Open grassy places and waste ground. March-October. 15-30 cm.

▼ Ragwort
Roadsides, waste ground, grassy places. Flowerheads in flat-topped clusters. June-October. 30-150 cm

Rape ▶
Roadsides and fields. May-August. Up to 1m.

▲ Wild Pansy
Grassy places and cornfields. Flowers can also be all yellow, all violet, or pink and white. April-September. 15-45 cm.

▼ Gorse
Heaths and commons. March-July. 60-200 cm.

▼ Viper's Bugloss

Waysides and sand dunes. Sharp hairs on stems. Bristly leaves. Rare in Scotland. June-September. 30-90 cm.

Common Forget-me-Not ▶

Roadsides, fields, and open grassy places. April-September. 15-30 cm.

◀ Sea Aster

Saltmarshes. Petals can also be white. July-October. 1 m.

◀ Common Speedwell

Grassy places and woods. May-August. 10-40 cm.

Common Milkwort ▶

Heaths, dunes, grassy places. May-September. 10-30 cm.

▼ Brooklime

In and by ponds, streams and other wet places. May-September. 20-60 cm.

Lesser Periwinkle ▶

Woods and hedgebanks. March-May. Flowering stems up to 15 cm.

Bugle ▶

Damp woods and grassy places. Has creeping runners. Leaves are often purplish. May-July. 10-30 cm.

Harebell ▼

Dry grasslands and heaths. Called Bluebell in Scotland. Locally common throughout Britain. July-August. 15-40 cm.

▲ Bluebell

Woods and hedgebanks. Flowers can also be white or pink. April-June. 20-50 cm.

▲ Honeysuckle
Climbing in woods, scrub and hedges. Fruits ripen to red in autumn. June-September. Up to 6 m.

▲ Dog Rose
Hedges and woods. Flowers may be pink or white. Rarer in Scotland. June-July. 1-3 m.

▼ Greater Bindweed
Hedgerows, walls, waste places. Less common in the North. July-September. 1-3 m.

▼ Bistort
Meadows and grassy roadsides, often near water. More common in northern England. June-August. 25-50 cm.

▼ Knotgrass
Waste ground, fields and seashores. A low, far-spreading plant. July-October. Creeping stems 3-200 cm.

Great Willowherb ►
Ditches, marshes, near streams. Rare in northern Scotland. July-August. 80-150 cm.

◄ Sea Bindweed
Sandy beaches; sometimes shingle. Rare in Scotland. June-August. Trailing stems up to 50 cm.

▼ Sand Spurrey
Sandy or gravelly places. Leaves end in a small bristle. May-September. 5-25 cm.

▲ Sea Milkwort
Grassy saltmarshes. Creeping stems. June-August. 10-30 cm tall.

◄ Thrift
Rocky cliffs near coast; mountains inland. March-October. 5-30 cm.

Common Centuary ▶
Grassland, dunes and woods. Rarer in Scotland. June-October. 2-50 cm.

◀ Heather or Ling
Heaths and moors. Flowers can also be white. Leaves overlap. July-September. Up to 60 cm.

▲ Rosebay Willowherb
Waste ground, roadsides. Seed has a hairy "parachute". July-September. 30-120 cm.

Bell Heather ▶
Dry heaths and moors. Not common in Midlands. July-September. Up to 60 cm.

▲ Herb Robert
Woods and hedgebanks. Fruit has a long "beak". May-September. 10-30 cm.

▼ Bilberry

Heaths, moors and woods. Blue-black berries. Flowers April-June. Up to 60 cm.

Ragged Robin ▲

Damp meadows, marshes, woods. Sepals form a tube. May-June. 30-75 cm.

Lady's Smock ▼

Damp meadows and near streams. Flower can be pink or white and lilac. April-June. 15-60 cm.

▲ Lesser Knapweed

Grassland and waysides. Stem is grooved below flowerhead. June-September. 15-60 cm.

◄ Hemp Agrimony
Damp places. Local to rare in Scotland. July-September. 30-120 cm.

▲ Policeman's Helmet
River banks, waste places, and near streams. Rare in some areas. July-October. 1-2 m.

Foxglove ►
Open woods, hedgerows, heaths. Poisonous. June-September. 50-150 cm.

▼ Valerian
Scrub, woods and grassy places. June-August. 20-150 cm.

◄ Red Campion
Woodlands and hedgerows. Rare in some areas. May-June. 30-90 cm.

◀ Watermint
Near water, marshes, damp woods.
July-October. 15-90 cm.

Early Purple Orchid ▶
Woods and copses. Locally common throughout Britain.
May-June. 15-60 cm.

◀ Wild Teasel
Roadsides, woodland edges, near streams.
July-August. 50-200 cm.

◀ Devil's Bit Scabious
Wet grassy places.
June-October.
15 -100 cm.

▲ Field Scabious
Dry grassland, waste places. June-September. 15-80 cm.

Common Dog Violet ▶
Hedgerows and woods.
April-July.
5-20 cm.

Tufted Vetch ▼

Climbs on other plants in hedges and grassy places. June-August. Flowers 10 mm long.

▲ Ivy-leaved Toadflax

Old walls, occasionally rocks. Often forms clumps. May-September. Flowers 10 mm long.

Sea Lavender ▼

Muddy saltmarshes. Often forms large mats. Not in northern Scotland. July-October. 8-30 cm.

▲ Woody Nightshade

Hedges, woods, waste places. Poisonous. Not common in Scotland. June-September. Scrambling stems 30-200 cm.

▲ Scarlet Pimpernel

Cultivated and waste ground. A sub-species has small blue flowers. Rarer in Scotland. June-August. 6-30 cm.

▼ Long-headed Poppy

Corn and other fields and waste ground. Longer capsule and paler petals than Field Poppy. June-July. 20-60 cm.

◀ Field Poppy

Corn and other fields, waste ground. Rare in northern Scotland. June-August. 20-60 cm.

▼ Wood Woundwort

Woods, hedgebanks, waste ground. July-August. 30-100 cm.

◄ Greater Stitchwort
Woods, hedgerows and roadsides. Large petals are split to about half-way. April-June. 15-60 cm.

▲ Wood Anemone
Woods. Often forms carpets. Flowers have up to nine petal-like sepals. March-May. 6-30 cm.

Wood Garlic ▼
Damp woods. Not common in northern Scotland. April-June. 10-25 cm.

◄ Garlic Mustard
Hedges and woods. Not common in northern Scotland. April-June. 20-120 cm.

Dog's Mercury ▲
Woodlands. Not common in northern Scotland. February-April. 15-20 cm.

▼ White Bryony

Climbs in hedges and scrub. Berries are poisonous. Rarer in Scotland. May-September. Up to 4 m.

▼ Wild Strawberry

Woods and scrubland. Leaves have three leaflets. Can cover large patches. April-July.

Cow Parsley ▼

Hedgebanks, roadsides, ditches. Leaves are divided into feathery segments. April-June. 60-100 cm.

▼ Upright Hedge Parsley

Roadsides, grassy places. Flowers later than Cow Parsley, and leaves less feathery. July-August. 50-125 cm.

▼ Meadowsweet
Marshes, water meadows and near ditches. Flowers smell sweet. May-September 60-120 cm.

▲ Water Crowfoot
Ponds, streams and ditches. May-June. Flowers are 10-20 mm across.

Wild Carrot ▶
Grassy places, especially near the sea. June-August. 30-100 cm.

Hogweed ▲
Open woods, roadsides, grassy places. June-September. 50-200 cm.

Daisy ▲
Short grassland, especially lawns. March-October. 3-12 cm.

▲ Nettle

Waysides, waste ground, woods. Has stinging hairs. June-August. 30-150 cm.

▼ White Dead Nettle

Roadsides, hedgerows and waste ground. Rare in north Scotland. May-December. 20-60 cm.

▲ Shepherd's Purse

Waysides and waste ground. Flowers all year. 3-40 cm.

▼ White Clover

Garden lawns, grassy places. June-September. Upright stems up to 25 cm.

◄ White Campion

Waysides, hedgebanks, waste ground. Sticky hairs. May-September. 30-100 cm.

◄ Bladder Campion

Roadsides and grassy places. Usually hairless. June-August. 25-90 cm.

◄ Sea Campion

Sea cliffs, shingle beaches. Smaller than Bladder Campion, with broader petals. June-August. 8-25 cm.

▼ Chickweed

Fields, waste places, gardens. Flowers all year. 5-40 cm.

▲ Corn Spurrey

Cornfields, cultivated land. June-August. 7-40 cm.

Yarrow ▲
Waste ground and grassy places. June-August. 8-45 cm.

▲ Ox-eye Daisy
Grassy places and roadsides. Upper leaves are toothed. June-August. 20-70 cm.

Sea Sandwort ►
Sand and shingle beaches. May-August. 5-25 cm.

▼ Pellitory-of-the-wall
Wall and rock crevices. Not in northern Scotland. June-October. 30-100 cm.

▲ Wood Sorrel
Woods and hedgebanks. Flowers close at night and in bad weather. Petals have lilac veins. April-May. 5-15 cm.

▲ Black Nightshade
Cultivated and waste ground. Rare in Scotland. July-September. Up to 60 cm.

▲ Bramble
Woods, scrubland, hedges, open ground. May-September. Arching stems up to 5 m.

▼ Greater Plantain
Cultivated land, waysides, lawns. Broad leaves. May-September. 10-15 cm.

▲ Ribwort Plantain
Grassy and waste places, lawns. Ribbed leaves. April-August. Up to 45 cm.

Butterflies

♀

Wall Brown ♂

▲ Wall Brown
Woodlands and rough, open ground. Often rests on walls. Not in northern Scotland. Seen March-September. 44-46 mm.

♂

Grayling ♀

▲ Grayling
Sandy places, chalk downs. Less common in Wales and East Anglia. Seen July-August. 56-61 mm.

♂

Meadow Brown ♀

▲ Meadow Brown
Meadows and other grassy places. Less common in Scotland. Seen June-September. 50-55 mm.

Small Heath ▶
Many areas including open woods, marshes and dry hillsides. Seen April-September. 33-35 mm.

Painted Lady ▶
Dry, open places. Likes thistles. Seen June-October. 62-65 mm.

Painted Lady

Red Admiral ▶
Gardens and woodland edges. Migrant from North Africa. Seen May-October. 66-68 mm.

▲ Small Tortoiseshell
Gardens and open places. Less widespread in Wales and Scotland. Seen April-November. 48-52 mm.
▼

Small Tortoiseshell

▲ Peacock
Gardens. Not present in northern Scotland. Seen August-October. 62-68 mm.

▲ Orange Tip

Woodland edges and hedgerows. Not in parts of Scotland. Seen April-June. 42-48 mm.

▼

Orange Tip

▲ Common Blue

Prefers downs and rough meadows. Seen April-September. 28-36 mm.

Common Blue

▼ Small Copper

All types of country. Less widespread in Scotland. Seen May-September. 26-30 mm.

▲ Large White

Woods, gardens and open places. Caterpillar eats brassicas. Seen May-August. 62-64 mm.

Large White ♀

Brimstone ♂

▲ Brimstone

Hedges, gardens and woodland paths. Adult hibernates. Not in Scotland. Seen June-September. 58-60 mm.

▼ Small White

Gardens and other cultivated places. Less widespread in Scotland. Seen May-August. 48-50 mm.

▼ Green-veined White

Open woodland and grassy places, gardens. Caterpillar eats leaves and seed-pods of Garlic Mustard. Seen May-September. 47-50 mm.

Seashore

◀ Gut Laver
A seaweed found in pools on upper and middle shores and estuaries. 20 cm long.

◀ Sea Lettuce
A seaweed found on middle and lower levels of rocky shores. 20 cm across.

Bladder Wrack ▲
A seaweed of rocky shores. Up to 60 cm long.

◀ Channelled Wrack
A seaweed found on rocks of the upper shore. 10 cm tall.

▼ Bread-crumb Sponge
On rocks, shells and seaweed holdfasts. 10 cm across.

▲ Haliclona oculata
A sponge found on lower shores in fast currents and estuaries with muddy gravel. Up to 16 cm long.

Sea Oak ▶
A seaweed found in pools, on stalks of other seaweeds and on rocks. 20 cm tall.

▼ Beadlet Anemone

Rock pools at most levels of the shore. 5 cm high.

▼ Snakelocks Anemone

Rocky shores. Not on east or south-east coasts. Can be grey or greenish. 10 cm across.

▲ Daisy Anemone

In rock crevices or mud of shallow pools. 10 cm high.

Dahlia Anemone

▲ Dahlia Anemone

In crevices in rock pools. 15 cm high when open.

◀ Hermit Crab Anemone

On mollusc shells inhabited by Hermit Crab. 10 cm high.

◀ Common Hermit Crab

Mostly lower shore, in rock pools. 5-10 cm long.

▲ Common Limpet
On rocky shores, attached to rocks. 7 cm long.

▲ Common Periwinkle
On rocky and muddy shores. 2.5 cm high.

▲ Netted Dog Whelk
On mud and gravel off shore and on lower shore. 2.5 cm high.

▲ Saddle Oyster
On lower shore, attached to rocks. 6 cm wide.

▲ Common Whelk
Lower shore of rocky or sandy beaches. 8 cm high.

▲ Slipper Limpet
Low water and off shore, often attached to one another. 4-5 cm long.

▲ Common Mussel
Rocky shores, pier piles and estuaries. 1-10 cm long.

▲ Dog Whelk
On rocks and in crevices of lower shore. 3 cm high.

▲ Painted Topshell
On rocks and under stones on lower shore. 2.5 cm high.

▲ Common Oyster
Shallow and deep water. 10-15 cm long.

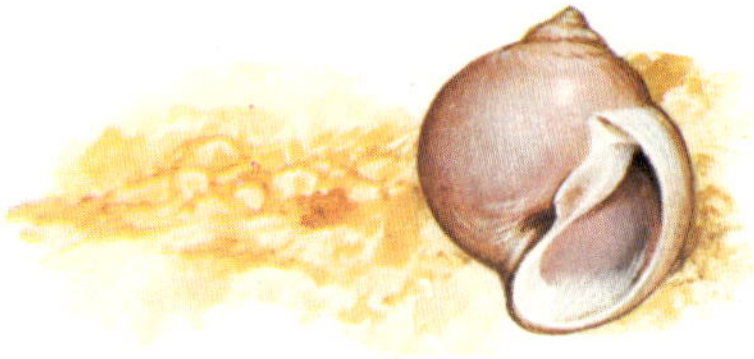

▲ **Necklace Shell**
Sandy shores. 3 cm high.

▲ **Razor Shell**
Burrows in mud. 12 cm long.

▲ **Common Sand Gaper**
Burrows in muddy sand on lower shore. 12 cm wide.

▲ **Edible Cockle**
In mud and sand of middle shore and below. 4 cm across.

▲ **Rayed Trough Shell**
Sand or gravel on lower shores. 5 cm long.

▲ **Baltic Tellin**
In mud and sand of seashores and estuaries. 2 cm long.

▲ **Horse Mussel**
From lower shore to deep water. 20 cm long.

▲ **Flat Periwinkle**
Under brown seaweed on rocky shores. 1 cm high.

▼ Brittle Stars

Under stones on lower shore. Small Brittle Star 3 cm across. Common Brittle Star 3-8 cm across.

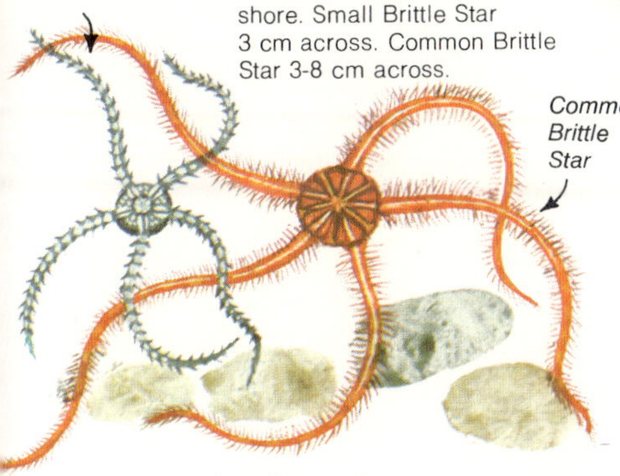

◀ Common Starfish

On the shore, 5-10 cm across; in deep water, up to 50 cm.

Sunstar ▼

In shallow water, lower shore. Up to 15 cm.

Sea Potato ▶

Burrows deep in sand of lower shore. 5-6 cm long.

▼ Edible Sea Urchin

Lower rocky shores and off shore. 15 cm across.

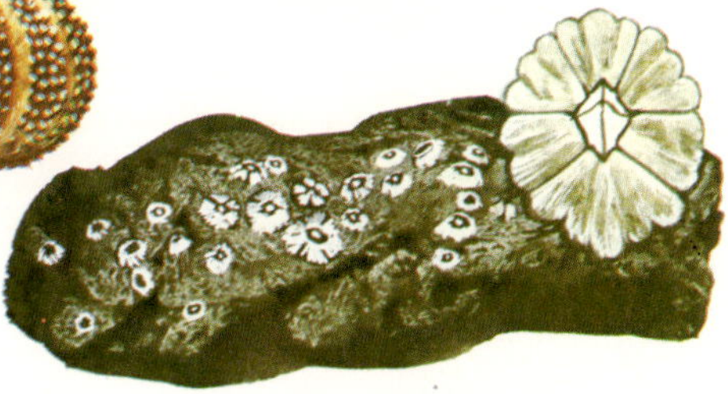

Acorn Barnacle ▶

On rocky shores. 5 mm long.

▼ Star Barnacle

On rocks of upper shore. 1 cm long.

▲ Moon Jellyfish

On all kinds of coasts. 15 cm across.

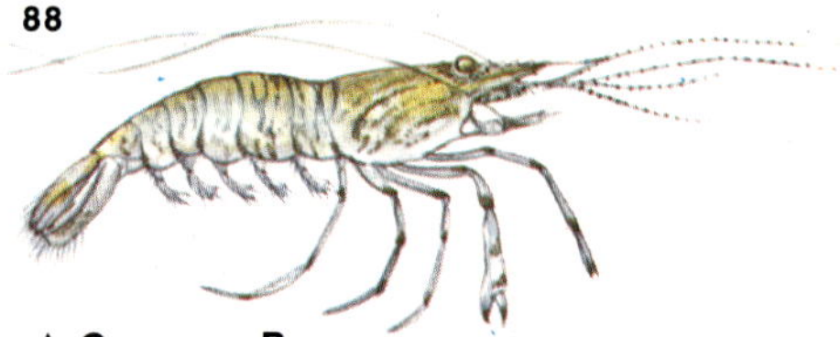

▲ Common Prawn
Shallow water and rock pools. 5-8 cm long.

▲ White Shrimp
Rock pools on lower shore; shallow waters of estuaries. 5 cm long.

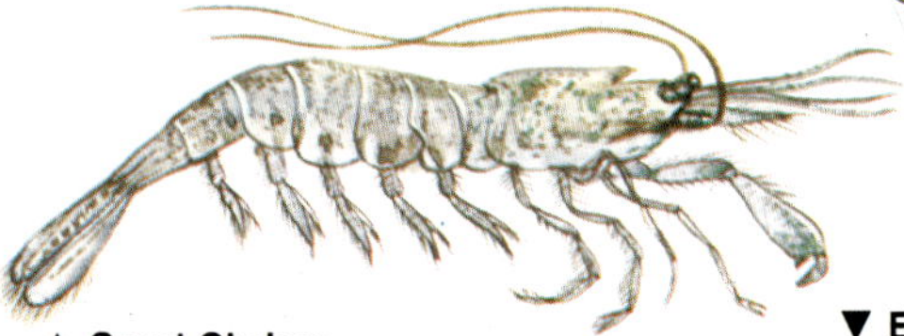

▲ Sand Shrimp
Sand estuaries. 5 cm long.

▲ Shore Crab
Sandy, muddy and rocky shores; estuaries. 8 cm across.

▲ Broad-clawed Porcelain Crab
Under stones on middle and lower shores. 1.2 cm across.

▼ Common Lobster
Only small ones in rock pools of lower shore. Can grow up to 45 cm long elsewhere.

▼ Montagu's Plated Lobster
Under seaweed and stones of lower shore. 4-6 cm long.

▼ Edible Crab
Only small ones in rock pools in lower shore. Can grow up to 11.5 cm long elsewhere.

▲ Common Cuttlefish
In sheltered bays and washed up dead on strand line. 30 cm long.

Trees

▲ **Scots Pine**
Often in plantations. Needles are in pairs. Bark flakes off in "plates"

◀ **Norway Spruce**
Prickly needles. Small brown buds. Peg-like bumps left on twigs when needles are pulled off.

▲ **Maritime Pine**
Often in plantations. Rare in Scotland. Needles are in pairs. Long bud. Long, bare trunk.

▲ **Sitka Spruce**
Less common in eastern England. Prickly needles. Plump yellow buds. Yellow twigs.

▼ European Larch

Deciduous. Bunches of soft, light green needles leave small knobs on twigs when they fall.

▲ Douglas Fir

Soft, fragrant needles. Cones have three-pointed bracts on each scale.

▼ European Silver Fir

Rare in east and south-east England. Needles are green above, silvery below.

▲ Corsican Pine

Often in plantations. Needles are in pairs. Onion-shaped buds.

▲ Juniper

Needles are in threes with white band on upper surface. Berry-like cones.

▼ Yew

Often planted in churchyards. Leaves and berries are poisonous.

▲ Chile Pine

Also called Monkey Puzzle. Stiff, leathery leaves with sharp points.

▼ English Oak

Less common in northern Scotland. Acorns have long stalks. Leaves are short-stalked.

▼ Common Ash

Less common in northern Scotland. Seeds are in clusters called "keys".

Seeds

Flowers

▼ Rowan

Clusters of flowers appear in May. Berries ripen in August.

▲ Common Alder

Always found near water. Reddish catkins ripen to cone-like fruits.

Fruit

Acorn

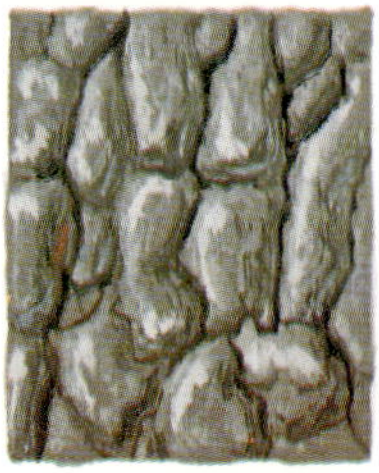

▲ Sessile Oak

Acorn is usually stalkless. Leaves are long-stalked.

▼ Aspen

Often grows in thickets. Leaves tremble in the wind. White downy catkins appear in May on female trees.

▲ Goat Willow

Common on damp waste ground and in scrub woodland. Catkins, known as Pussy Willows, appear in late winter.

▼ White Willow

Common by water. Not in north-west Scotland. Weeping Willow is a variety of this species.

▲ Silver Birch

Catkins, known as "lamb's tails", are yellow with pollen in April. Bark peels off in ribbons.

▼ English Elm

Many have been killed by Dutch Elm disease. Clusters of red flowers appear before leaves.

▲ Sycamore

Paired, winged seeds twist as they fall. Bark becomes scaly.

▲ Common Lime

Yellowish-green flowers appear in July. Fruits hang from leafy wing.

▲ Common Beech

Leaves turn copper-brown in autumn. Nuts are triangular, encased in a husk.

▲ Horse Chestnut
Less common in Scotland. "Candles" of flowers (white or pink) appear in May.

▼ Sweet Chestnut
Flowers appear in June. Edible chestnuts are encased in a prickly fruit.

▲ Holly
Less common in northern Scotland. Evergreen. Berries found only on female trees.

▲ Common Hawthorn
Grows in thickets and hedgerows. Berries usually have only one stone.

The leaves and bark of each of the species shown below are illustrated on page 89–95.

Places to Visit

This section describes a large selection of places to observe wildlife in Cumbria and Lancashire (including South Lancashire and the adjacent coastline of Northern Merseyside). The sites listed include good examples of the habitats described in the beginning of the book and also nature reserves, country parks, birdwatching areas, museums, zoos and gardens.

The descriptions of the places to visit are grouped by county in alphabetical order. Sites situated within the Lake District National Park are listed in a separate section under Cumbria. Sites in Northern Merseyside are included under Lancashire. Each place is marked by a number on a map which appears at the beginning of each section. The Pennine Way is also marked but is not numbered; it is described immediately below the map of Cumbria.

The descriptions outline the main points of interest at each place and give some idea of the plants and animals which may be found there. They also give details about location and approach by road. Where relevant, telephone numbers and general restrictions on opening times are also included. To avoid disappointment, the visitor is advised to check these in advance, as in some cases, opening hours are irregular and liable to change. Details of opening times for Bank Holidays and the Christmas period are not always given.

In most cases the Ordnance Survey (1:500 000) map number and grid reference are given, at the very end of the description (eg. OS 142: 205 890). The sheet number follows after "OS" and the grid reference after the colon. With large areas such as forests and estuaries the reference given is often for a car park or a point of access; where a square reference is given (eg. OS 142: 20 89) this indicates the approximate centre of the area.

The visitor to nature reserves is reminded that the reserve exists to protect the habitat and its wildlife. Great care should therefore be taken on reserves, and any conditions and restrictions strictly adhered to. For some reserves a permit may have to be obtained in advance. This is indicated where it applies together with details of where to obtain permission. (See also the Country Code and points about nature conservation on page 118.)

Further information about the sites listed, and other places of interest in this area can be obtained locally and by consulting the relevant Ordnance Survey map. The English Tourist Board and Lake District National Park Authorities publish a range of literature on the region which can be obtained from their Information Centres (see page 119).

Most of the nature trails and forest walks have an accompanying booklet or leaflet. If these publications are not available on site, an address from which they can be obtained is given, either at the end of the entry or on page 119.

Cumbria

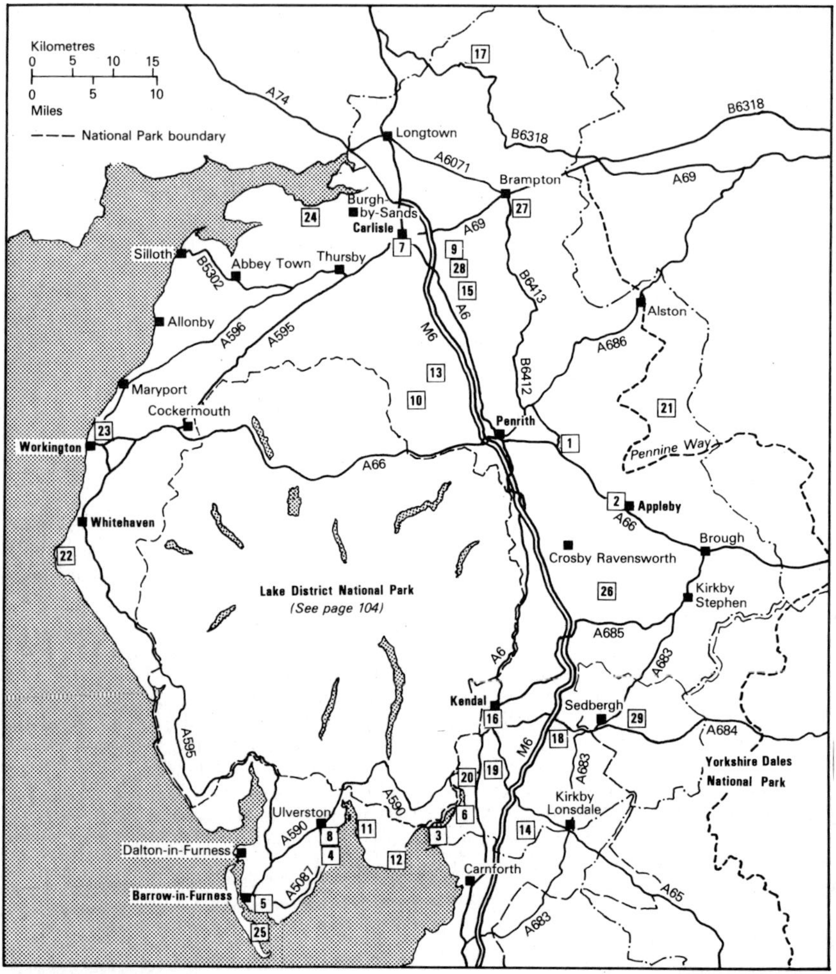

Pennine Way

Long distance footpath 250 miles/402 km long, from the Peak District to the Scottish Border, passing through three National Parks. The section of the Pennine Way in Cumbria offers some spectacular scenery and interesting changes in geology. The walk from Caldron Snout to High Cup Nick (see page 12) is considered one of the most exciting parts of the route. The path continues to Cross Fell, the highest peak in the Pennines, with views over the Eden Valley, Lake District and Solway Firth. Please remember that the Pennine Way is a high level route, some of it over rough country and is often subject to bad weather conditions, particularly around Cross Fell; attention should be paid to hill safety (see page 119). An excellent book, with maps, is *The Pennine Way* by Tom Stephenson published for the Countryside Commission by HMSO. OS 86, 87 and 91.

1 Acorn Bank
Gardens. National Trust. Spring bulbs, walled garden with herbaceous plants and herb garden.
□Open daily excluding Monday, end of April–September. 6 miles/9.5 km east of Penrith on A66, just north of Temple Sowerby. OS 91: 612 281.

2 Appleby Castle
Rare breeds of farm animals, such as Chillingham and Longhorn cattle, Manx Loghtan, Soay and Jacob sheep, Tamworth and Gloucester Old Spot pigs and Bagot goats. Also large collection of wildfowl, including Red-breasted Goose, Hooded Merganser, Black Swan and Red-crested Pochard, selection of pheasants and owls. Grounds attract a variety of wild birds; all three species of woodpecker, Buzzard, Sparrowhawk, Pied Flycatcher, Waxwing and Crossbill have been seen. Guide book and leaflets, shop, cafe, picnic areas, woodland walk and nature trail.
□Tel: Appleby 51402. Open daily, Easter–end of September. OS 91: 685 200.

3 Arnside Knott
National Trust. Area of limestone grassland and woodland, with fine views over Morecambe Bay to hills of Lake District. Limestone plants include Columbine, Squinancywort, Blue Fleabane, Dark Red and Broad-leaved Helleborine, Rockrose, Common Milkwort and Dropwort. Interesting insect population with Glow Worms and a number of less common butterflies and moths. Tits, warblers, Goldcrest, Treecreeper, Great Spotted and Green Woodpeckers in woods. Red Squirrel and Slow Worm may also be seen. Nature trail leaflet available from National Trust Regional Office, Broadlands, Borrans Road, Waterhead, Ambleside (Tel: Ambleside 3003).
□7 miles/11 km north-west of Carnforth on unclassified road via Silverdale, turn west at top of Red Hill. OS 97: 456 774.

4 Bardsea Country Park
Cumbria County Council. Strip of coastland with shingle and mudflats, and 60 acres/24 ha of Oakwood. Coast provides good birdwatching areas for waders and wildfowl. Wood contains Wood Anemone, Primrose, Daffodil and Wild Cherry. Footpaths and picnic area.
□2 miles/3 km south of Ulverston on A5087, main car park down Cooper Lane. OS 96 & 97: 299 740.

5 Barrow Docks
Dockland. Good for birds in winter, especially in hard weather. Cavendish Dock best. Pochard, Tufted Duck, Goldeneye, Wigeon and Mute Swan often seen. Occasionally less common species such as Smew, Long-tailed Duck, Scaup and Red-necked and Slavonian Grebes.
□Some of the docks are private, but most of the area can be viewed from public roads. Follow A590 from centre of Barrow-in-Furness, third road left after bridge also goes to docks. Or follow A5087, after sharp left-hand turn, cross railway then follow one of streets on right. OS 96: 213 682.

6 Beachwood, Arnside
Nature reserve. Cumbria Naturalists' Trust. Small area of meadow and mixed woodland with great diversity. Flowers include Daffodil, Wood Garlic, Early Purple and Common Spotted Orchids, Common Bistort, Betony, Herb Paris, Solomon's-Seal, Green Hellebore, Spurge Laurel, Lily of the Valley and White Butterbur. Good variety of insects including Brimstone butterfly. Common woodland birds, with ducks and waders on the estuary. Please keep to the footpaths.
□5½ miles/9 km north-west of Carnforth. Park at Arnside promenade, walk in south-west direction along shore for about 500 yards/450 metres. OS 97: 452 786.

7 Carlisle Museum and Art Gallery
Fine natural history section with an extensive collection of British birds shown in natural settings; British mammals including Pine Marten, Polecat and Wild Cat. Fine geological displays and collection of Cumbrian archaelogical exhibits.
□Tullie House, Castle Street (Tel: Carlisle 34781). Open April–September daily except Sunday; June–August, Sunday afternoon also.

8 Conishead Priory
Grounds of old priory close to Morecambe Bay, with three nature trails: *American Garden Wood* – cedars, redwoods and Noble Fir with shrub layer of Rhododendron and Snowberry, many woodland birds; *The Shore* – good for waders, wildfowl, gulls and terns; *The Beechwood* – Ash, Elm, Oak, Corsican and Scots Pine, fungi in autumn. Leaflet available.
☐Ulverston (Tel: Ulverston 54019). Open Saturday and Sunday afternoons, Easter–September. 2 miles/3 km south of Ulverston on A5087. OS 96 & 97: 30 75.

9 Corby Castle
Castle with grounds by River Eden; fine trees.
☐Great Corby, Near Wetheral, Carlisle (Tel: Carlisle 60246). Open daily April–October. 4 miles/6.5 km south-east of Carlisle, take unclassified road south off A69 for Great Corby, immediately east of Warwick Bridge.

10 Greystoke Forest
Forestry Commission. Coniferous forest with bothy (hut) and observation hide in conservation area in heart of forest.
☐For use of hide and bothy apply to Head Forester, Millfield Lodge, Hutton Roof, Penrith. 10 miles/16 km west of Penrith, turn north off B5288 at Greystoke village. OS 90: 39 33.

11 Holker Hall and Park
Gardens. Fine example of Monkey Puzzle tree, said to be oldest in Britain, some unusual conifers. Best in early summer. Deer park with Red, Sika and Fallow Deer; wild Roe Deer in woods. Countryside museum and aquarium, cafe, shop.
☐Cark-in-Cartmel, Near Grange-over-Sands (Tel: Flookburgh 328). Open daily excluding Saturdays, April–end of September. 4 miles/6.5 km west of Grange-over-Sands on B5277, turn north onto B5278 at Flookburgh. OS 96 & 97: 360 774.

12 Humphrey Head
Limestone grassland which protrudes out into Morecambe Bay. Steep cliffs on east side with areas of scrub and saltmarsh on west; Head itself surrounded by intertidal sandflats. Number of unusual plants such as Alpine Cinquefoil, Goldilocks, Portland Spurge, Bloody Cranesbill, Milk Vetch and Rock Samphire. Good wader roosts; winter wildfowl include large flocks of Wigeon, Pintail, Greylag and Pink-footed Geese.
☐Public right of way on head, beware of quicksands and tidals channels. 3 miles/5 km south of Grange-over-Sands, from Flookburgh Square take road south, then first turning left, keep right for 2 miles/3 km, park on shore. OS 96 & 97: 392 733.

13 Hutton-in-the-Forest
House dating from fourteenth century onwards, and gardens with specimen trees and ornamental lake. Good for wild plants and other wildlife.
☐Penrith (Tel: Skelton 207). Open mid May–September, Thursdays and Bank Holidays, afternoons only; in winter, by appointment only. 7 miles/11 km north-west of Penrith; turn off M6 at Catterlen onto B5305. OS 90: 460 358.

14 Hutton Roof and Clawthorpe Fell
Extensive area of limestone pavement with typical plants (see page 18).
☐4 miles/6 km north-east of Carnforth along A6070; at Clawthorpe take unclassified road towards Hutton Roof. About 1½ miles/2 km along this road are public footpaths, west to Clawthorpe Fell and east to Hutton Roof. OS 97: 553 789.

15 Inglewood, High Stand
Forestry Commission. Mixed woodland with streams and ponds. Variety of woodland birds; wildfowl may be seen in winter. Hides for watching Roe Deer.
☐Permit required for observation hides, apply to Local Forester, High Stand Office, Armathwaite, Near Carlisle, Cumbria (Tel: Wetheral 60363). 8 miles/13 km south-east of Carlisle, turn east off A6 at Low Hesket. OS 86: 486 478.

16 Kendal Museum
Large collection of mammals from all over the world. Lake District natural history exhibitions; diaramas showing lowland to mountain top habitats around Kendal.

□Station Road (Tel: Kendal 21374). Open daily, all year; Saturday and Sunday, afternoons only.

17 Kershope Forest, Border Forest Park
Forestry Commission. The Border Forest Park is the largest expanse of forest in the British Isles. As well as coniferous plantations there are areas of open moorland and high hill ranges with excellent views over northern England and southern Scotland. Kershope Forest lies in the north-east corner of Cumbria. Previously used for sheep grazing it is now an area of plantations, mainly spruce and pine, with some areas of moorland. Many woodland and moorland birds. Roe Deer are common and Wild Goats may be seen in the more remote moorland areas.
□Information and displays on the Border Forest Park is available from Kielder Castle Visitor Centre (Tel: Kielder 50209), open during the summer. OS 79, 80 & 86.

18 Killington Reservoir
Large flocks of Goosander in winter, also Wigeon and Teal. Small breeding population of wildfowl.
□6 miles/10 km east of Kendal, turn south off A684 for Killington village. Reservoir can also be seen from Killington Lake service station on M6. OS 97: 59 91.

19 Lancaster-Kendal Canal Nature Trail
Cumbria Naturalists' Trust. Trail along bank of canal; meanders through drumlin landscape (small hummocks formed by glacial drift). Meadowsweet, Angelica and Watermint along canal banks; Maidenhair Fern on bridges; Curly Pondweed, Spiked Milfoil, Spineless Hornwort, Water Plantain and Bur-reed in the water. Birds present include Mute Swan, warblers, Reed Bunting, Grey Wagtail, Dipper and Kingfisher. Snails on bridges. Leaflet available from Cumbria Naturalists' Trust, Rydal Road, Ambleside.
□4½ miles/ 7 km south of Kendal. East off A591 to Stainton, car park just over canal. OS 97: 521 855.

20 Levens Hall and Levens Park
Elizabethan house; seventeenth century topiary garden, still laid out to original plan. Levens Park, one of the oldest landscaped parks in England, has a fine Oak avenue and good specimen trees; Bagot goats and herd of black Fallow Deer. River Kent flows through park.
□Near Kendal (Tel: Sedgwick 60321). House and gardens open Easter–September; House, Tuesday–Thursday, Sunday and Bank Holidays, afternoons only; gardens open daily. Access to park at all times. 5 miles/8 km south of Kendal along A6, near junction with A590. OS 97; 495 850.

21 Moorhouse National Nature Reserve
Nature Conservancy Council. Typical example of north Pennine moorland dominated by heathers, Cotton Grass and *Sphagnum* mosses. Interesting species such as Grass of Parnassus and Hairy Stonecrop occur in the rich flushes. Limestone outcrops produce patches of rich grassland where Mossy Saxifrage and Spring Sandwort grow. Mountain species such as Roseroot, Hoary Whitlow-grass and Green Spleenwort also occur. The lichen-rich heath area is also of interest. Birds of the area include Golden Plover, Dunlin, Snipe, Curlew, with Common Sandpiper and Dipper along the streams, and Ring Ouzel among the rocky outcrops. Leaflet available.
□Permit required away from rights of way; apply to Regional Officer, Nature Conservancy Council, Blackwell, Bowness-on-Windermere (Tel: Windermere 5286). Pennine Way passes through the reserve and over to Cross Fell. 8 miles/13 km north of Appleby. OS 91: 74 32.

22 St Bees Head
RSPB. Sandstone cliffs, good for seabirds especially between April and August. Breeding Fulmars, Guillemots, Razorbills, Puffins and a few pairs of Black Guillemots; also Kittiwakes and Herring Gulls. Plants include Rock Samphire and Bloody Cranesbill.
□Access at all times along public footpath from St Bees and Sandwith villages. Park at sea front car park, St Bees, and follow path north along coast. OS 89: 939 145.

23 Siddick Pond Nature Reserve

Allerdale District Council. Residual basin of the River Derwent providing an attractive habitat for a wide variety of birds. Summer visitors include Reed, Grasshopper and Sedge Warblers, Whitethroat, Shoveler and Tufted Duck. In winter, Snipe, Bewick and Whooper Swans and several species of ducks may be seen. Migrants include Green and Wood Sandpiper, Greenshank and Black Tern. A large Starling roost in the reserve attracts predators such as Peregrine; Long-eared and Short-eared Owls also occur. For further information contact J. Callion, 2 The Cherries, Scawfield, High Harrington, Workington (Tel: Harrington 830651).

□Permit required; apply to Parks Superintendent, Solway House, Mossbay Road, Workington (Tel: Workington 4351). 1 mile/1.5 km north of Workington, east off A596. OS 89: 00 30.

24 South Solway Coast

Area of Outstanding Natural Beauty. Large area of sandflats internationally important for wildfowl and waders. Pink-footed and Barnacle Geese, Oystercatcher, Knot, Lapwing, Dunlin, Golden Plover, Ringed Plover and Bar-tailed Godwit all occur; ducks include Wigeon, Mallard, Teal, Pintail and Shelduck.

□Best areas for birdwatching are at: Moricambe Bay – north of Silloth along unclassified road to Skinburness, then walk to Grune Point, or follow unclassified road west off B5307 at Kirkbride towards Cardurnock; Eden Estuary – carry along unclassified road from Cardurnock along edge of Firth or walk out from Burgh-by-Sands. OS 85.

25 South Walney

Nature reserve. Cumbria Naturalists' Trust. Mainly sand and shingle with many gravel pits and ponds; also sand dunes, saltmarsh and grassland. Plants include Biting Stonecrop, Prickly Saltwort, Portland Spurge, Scentless Mayweed and Yellow Horned Poppy on the shingle; Oyster Plant, Sea Campion, Tricolour Pansy, Hound's-tongue and Sea Holly on the dunes. Glasswort, Sea Milkwort, two species of Sea Lavender and Sea Aster on the saltmarsh, with Sea Beet, Sea Rocket and Rock Samphire along the tide line and saltings. Large nesting colonies of Herring and Lesser Black-backed Gulls – 40,000 pairs. Oystercatcher, Ringed Plover and Shelduck also breed. Several hundred pairs of Eider Duck, most southerly breeding population on west coast. Good for seawatching – Gannet, shearwaters and skuas, as well as passing seaduck. Booklet, nature trail, Bird Observatory and Ringing Station.

□Access by permit only; available on site or in advance from the Warden, South Walney Nature Reserve, Coast Guard Cottages, South Walney, Barrow-in-Furness (Tel: Barrow 41066). Parties must book in advance. Closed Mondays excluding Bank Holidays. Island of Walney just off Furness Peninsula. From Barrow-in-Furness cross bridge to island, turn left along the Promenade and Ocean Road, bearing right at King Alfred Hotel, then fourth left along Carr Lane; continue straight on for about 5 miles/8 km to reserve. Park near cottages. OS 96: 215 620.

26 Sunbiggin Tarn

Small upland tarn fed by lime-rich water, with reedbeds and wetlands around edge. Large Black-headed Gull colony, also Curlew, Lapwing, various ducks and occasional grebes. Little Owl may be seen among old farm buildings along road north of tarn. Surrounding limestone hills are good for plants; some more acid areas occur where heathers grow. Sedges and rushes, also Grass of Parnassus, Lousewort, Early and Northern Marsh Orchids, Birdseye Primrose, Marsh Marigold, Bogbean, Northern Bedstraw, Butterwort, Sundew and Yorkshire Milkwort.

□No rights of access to tarn but birds can be watched from road. 4 miles/6.5 km north-east of Tebay, junction 38 on M6, from A685 turn north onto B6261, then north-east for Raisbeck, on reaching village turn right and second left, Sunbiggin is 2 miles/3 km farther on. OS 91: 677 077. Several rights of way across fells between

Orton and Great Asby, see OS map 91. Paths beginning at: opposite tarn up track leading to Sunbiggin OS 91: 674 077; from Sunbiggin OS 91: 657 087; from Orton, OS 91: 635 085; from High Barn, 1.5 km/2 miles along unclassified road from Great Asby to B6260, OS 91: 668 117.

27 Talkin Tarn Country Park

Cumbria County Council. Tarn surrounded by woodland and pasture. Flowers include Violets, Marsh Marigold, Wood Sorrel and Heath Spotted Orchid. A wide variety of woodland birds; also Swallow, Swift and House Martin in summer. Goosander, Tufted Duck, Whooper and Bewick Swans, Coot and gulls may be seen in winter.

□11 miles/17 km east of Carlisle, turn south at Brampton B6513, after 2 miles/ 3 km turn east for tarn. OS 86: 470 533.

28 Wetheral Woods

National Trust. Gorge of River Eden, fine caves in sandstone cliffs. Woodland birds and Dippers.

□4 miles/6.5 km east of Carlisle off B6263 at Wetheral. OS 86: 470 533.

29 Yorkshire Dales National Park

Contrast of rich green valleys and bare upland moors. Garsdale and Dentdale lie in Cumbria. Limestone pavements and grassland support many interesting ferns and wild flowers including Birdseye Primrose, Mountain Pansy and Dark Green Helleborine. Hay meadows contain Yellow Rattle and Ragged Robin. Woodland plants include Primrose, Herb Paris, Bloody Cranesbill and Early Purple Orchid. Typical birds of the fells are Red Grouse, Golden Plover, Curlew, Raven and Buzzard. Dipper, Common Sandpiper and Grey Wagtail may be seen along the streams.

□*National Park Office* (postal enquiries and publications) Colvend, Hebden Road, Grassington, Skipton, North Yorkshire (Tel: Grassington 752748).

□*National Park Centre* (displays, information, leaflets, town trail) 72 Main Street, Sedbergh (Tel: Sedbergh 20125). Open daily April–end of September. OS 97: 65 92.

□*Whernside Cave and Fell Centre* Residential Centre of the National Park with an international reputation for caving courses but also dealing with other aspects of the National Park such as conservation and wildlife. Facilities for field studies. Whernside Manor, Dent, Sedbergh (Tel: Dent 213). OS 98: 725 858.

Cumbria–Lake District National Park

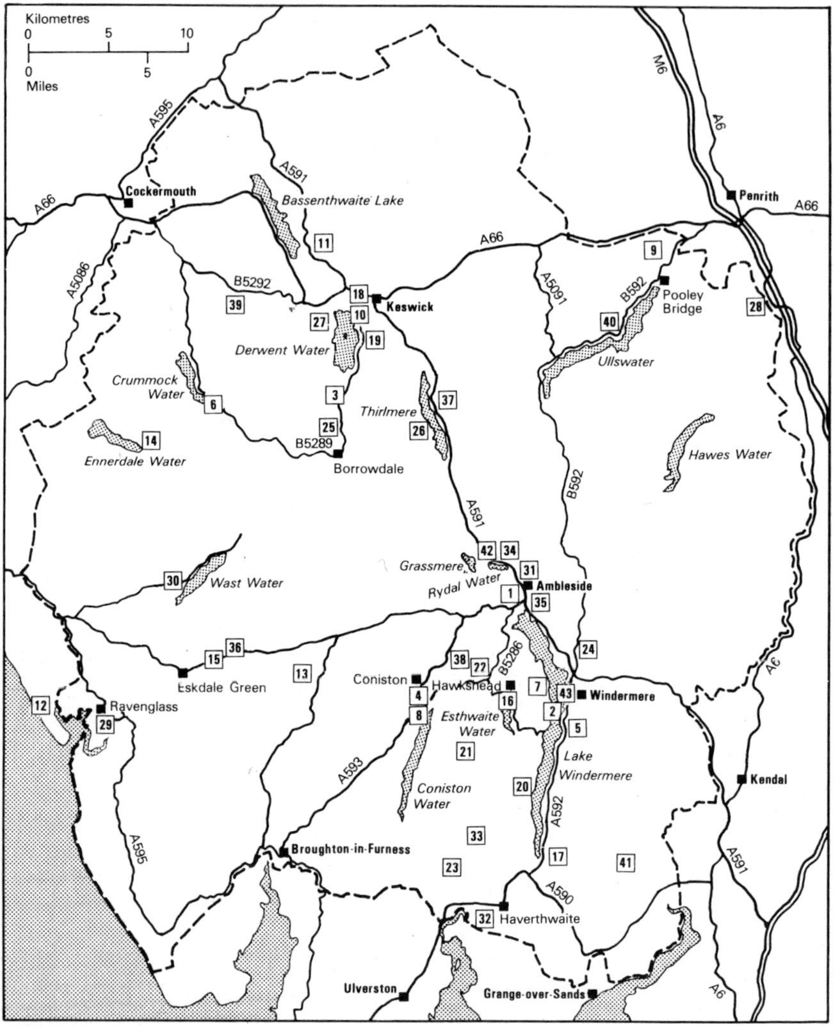

The Lake District National Park includes 880 square miles/2280 square km of mountains, valleys and lakes. Although much of the land is privately owned, there are hundreds of miles of footpaths both in the valleys and crossing the high fells. Land open to the public for car parks, picnicking, access to lake or river, or as woodland is nearly always clearly marked, as also are the footpaths where they leave the highway. Once on the fells you may walk or climb almost at will. A series of Walksheets is available from Brockhole, the National Park Visitor Centre (see 5), or from one of the Park Information Centres at Ambleside, Bowness, Coniston, Glenridding, Hawkshead, Pooley Bridge and Seatoller.

1 Ambleside

Market town at the head of Lake Windermere, surrounded by wooded hills. Stock Ghyll Force, a waterfall in a wooded gorge to the east of the town, has been a tourist attraction since Victorian times.

□*Day walk from Ambleside around Loughrigg Fell* (National Park Walksheet No W.1.) passes both Grasmere and Rydal Water, two of the more shallow lakes, good for wildlife.

□*National Park Information Centre* (leaflets, displays, Walksheets, relief map of lakes), Old Court House, Church Street (Tel: Ambleside 3084). Open daily, Easter–September.

□*National Trust Information Centre* (maps nature trails, leaflets), The Bridge House. Open daily, Easter–October.

2 Belle Isle

38 acre/15 ha island in Lake Windermere where Red-breasted Merganser breed. First completely round house built in England. Nature trail.

□(Tel: Windermere 3353). Open Monday, Tuesday, Thursday and Sunday, May–September. Motor launch leaves from end of Bowness promenade. OS 96 & 97: 394 967.

3 Borrowdale

Valley around River Derwent, south of Derwent Water, noted for its semi-natural woodland, especially rich in ferns, mosses, liverworts and lichens.

□*Three circular walks from Rosthwaite, in Borrowdale* (National Park Walksheet): Grange Fell; Castle Crag; Stonethwaite and Langstrathe Becks.

□*National Park Information Centre* (Illustrated talks, guided walks, Walksheets, study facilities and leaflets) Seatoller Barn, Daleshead Base (Tel: Borrowdale 294). Open daily, Easter–September. OS 89: 245 137.

4 Brantwood

Museum, garden and nature trail. Home of John Ruskin. Trail passes through Oakwoods, the tumbling falls of Beck Leven and onto the fells with views of Coniston Lake. Leaflet available.

□East of Lake Road, Coniston (Tel: Coniston 396 & 263). Open daily except Saturday, Easter–October. By appointment only, November–February. OS 96 & 97: 312 958.

5 Brockhole – Lake District National Park Visitor Centre

30 acres of gardens and woodland leading down to the shores of Lake Windermere. Lake shore walk; leaflet available. Mixed woodland containing Ash, Alder, Sycamore, Oak, Hazel, Holly, Hawthorn and Birch, while Herb Robert, Foxglove, Wild Angelica and Knapweed are just a few of the plants that form the groundcover; Globeflower grows along the lake shore. Woodland birds such as Treecreeper, tits and warblers are common; Red-breasted Merganser and Mallard on the lake, Common Sandpiper and Grey Wagtail along the shore; occasional Buzzard and Sparrowhawk. Red Squirrel in woods and Badger sometimes sighted in the vicinity ('Brockhole' meaning Badger sett). Exhibitions, displays, small reference library; theatre with talks and film displays daily, subjects include: Introducing Lakeland, Natural History, Wild Flowers, Farmers' Year, Old Industries, Hounds and Sheepdogs, Rocks and Landscape, Mines and Minerals. Shop with leaflets, books, maps etc. Cafe and picnic area. Launch trips on lake in summer.

□Brockhole, Windermere (Tel: Windermere 2231). Open daily late March–early November. Parties by appointment only. 2½ miles/4 km north of Windermere on A591. OS 90: 390 010.

6 Buttermere

Valley with varied landscape, ranging from wild crags at head of lake, to pastoral land around Buttermere village. Lake Buttermere and Crummock Water are owned by National Trust. Access to water and along much of the shores.

□*Three walks from Buttermere village* (National Park Walksheet No W. 4): lake shore; Rannerdale Knots (fine views); Scale Force.

□West of Borrowdale along B5289. OS 89: 17 16.

7 Claife Shore and Claife Heights

Lake Windermere shore walk. National Trust and Freshwater Biological Association. Plants include Wood Sanicle, Cuckoo Flower, Foxglove, Wood Garlic, Water Lobelia, Golden Saxifrage and Touch-me-not. Red and Roe Deer, Badger and Red Squirrel occasionally seen. Pied Flycatcher, Redstart, Red-breasted Merganser and Common Sandpiper just a few of the birds of the area. Leaflet available from National Trust Information Centres or Regional Office in Ambleside. Claife Heights (above the shore), also National Trust, is an upland area with some woodlands, mainly conifer plantations, and several small tarns. Deer, Red Squirrel and Badger are more likely to be seen here than along the shore. Several public footpaths. National Park Walksheet No. W.10 covers both these areas (available from National Park Information Centres).

□ West shore of Lake Windermere. For lake shore walk take ferry from Bowness, or B5285 from Hawkshead and park just before the Ferry House. OS 96 & 97: 388 957. One footpath across Claife Heights starts from Near Sawrey on B5285. OS 96 & 97: 371 957.

8 Coniston Water

One of the more gentle Lakeland areas with deciduous woods and fields sloping down to the shore. Public access round most of the shore, and on Torver Common, east of Torver.

□ *Three walks from Coniston* (National Park Walksheet No. W.4): around Mealy Gill; Tiberthwaite Gill and Yewdale woods; north shore of Coniston Water and Torver Beck.

□ *National Park Information Centre*, (leaflets on nature trails, guided walks etc.) Main Car Park, Coniston village. Open daily, Easter–September.

9 Dalemain

Medieval house with countryside museum, gardens and parkland with Fallow Deer.

□ Dacre, Pooley Bridge (Tel: Pooley Bridge 450). Open April–September, daily excluding Friday. OS 90: 477 269.

10 Derwent Water, Keswick

Shallow lake which attracts a variety of wintering wildfowl including Pochard, Tufted Duck and Red-breasted Merganser. One of only two lakes where a rare fish, the Vendace, occurs.

□ *Five walks from Keswick* (National Park Walksheet): shore of Derwent Water; Castlehead and Great Wood; Walla Crag; Falcon Cragg; Latrigg.

□ *National Park Information Centre*, (leaflets, displays, guided walks), Moot Hall, Market Place, Keswick (Tel: Keswick 72803). Open daily Easter–September.

□ *National Trust Information Centre* (leaflets, nature trails, maps, etc.), Lakeside, Keswick. Open daily, Easter–October.

11 Dodd Wood

Forest trail telling story of forestry. Forestry Commission. Coniferous wood with some Oaks around mill pond. Roe Deer, Red Squirrel, Buzzard and Sparrowhawk. Good views from Dodd summit. Leaflet available.

□ 4 miles/6.5 km north of Keswick on A591. OS 89: 235 282.

12 Drigg Dunes

Local nature reserve. Cumbria County Council. Sand dunes, saltmarsh and shingle. Carline Thistle, Marsh Felwort, Bloody Cranesbill, Yellow Horned Poppy and Portland Spurge on dunes; Glasswort, Sea Purslane and Sea Lavender on saltmarsh; and rare Isle of Man Cabbage on shingle. Large Black-headed Gull colony, other breeding birds include Sandwich, Common, Arctic and Little Terns, Shelduck, Red-breasted Merganser and Ringed Plover. Good variety of moths and butterflies; Small Copper, Meadow Brown, Small Tortoiseshell and Peacock Butterflies; look out for Cinnabar Moth caterpillars on Ragwort. Natterjack Toad and Adder. Leaflet available.

□ Access by permit only; apply to County Estate Surveyor and Valuer, Arroyo Block, The Castle, Carlisle (Tel: Carlisle 23456). Good views of major parts of estuary may be gained from village of Ravenglass. OS 96: 05 97.

13 Dunnerdale Forest
Forestry Commission. Coniferous and deciduous forest. Famous pack-bridge spans narrow gorge. Picnic site, several way-marked walks over fells start from picnic site.
□14 miles/22.5 km west of Ambleside, turn west off A593 onto unclassified road over Wrynose Pass. OS 96: 235 995.

14 Ennerdale Forest
Forestry Commission. Tree planting started in 1926 with Spruce, Larch and Scots Pine. Reafforestation has helped increase the populations of Roe Deer, Red Squirrel and Badger. Ennerdale Water is only lake in Lake District without a public road along its shores, so provides many quiet walks along some 16 miles/26 km of forest road. Leaflet 'Walking in Ennerdale Forest' available; picnic site. Two walks start from Bowness Knott car park.
□*Smithy Beck*. Forest trail. Japanese Larch and Scots Pine most common coniferous trees with native species such as Oak, Holly, Rowan and Hawthorn along Dry and Smithy Becks. Extreme northern limit of Holly Blue Butterfly. Good for mosses and lichens. Booklet available.
□*Nine Becks Walk*. 9 miles/14.5 km way-marked walk through forest following River Liza, particularly impressive after heavy rain.
□6 miles/10 km east of Cleator Moor, turn east off A5086 onto unclassified road via Croasdale and Ennerdale Bridge. Car park at end of Bowness Knott, OS 89: 108 155.

15 Eskdale
Valley in south-west of Lake District that can be seen from narrow-gauge Ravenglass and Eskdale Railway.
□*Three walks from Eskdale Terminus of the R & E Railway* (National Park Walksheet No. W.6.): Great Barrow and Eel Tarn; along the River Esk, Forge Bridge to Doctor Bridge; Hollinhead Crag and Blea Tarn. For terminus of railway (Dalegarth Station) take road eastwards from Eskdale Green. OS 89: 173 007.
□*Giggle Alley Walk*. Forestry Commission. Way-marked walk through old Beech and young Larch woodland. Starts from Eskdale Green, OS 89: 140 002.

16 Esthwaite Water.
The most nutrient-rich lake in the area. Good for plants; Water Lobelia, White and Yellow Water Lilies, Water Milfoils and rare pondweeds occur. Nesting birds include Great Crested and Little Grebes and Greylag Goose. Vegetation has been extensively studied at North Fen National Nature Reserve, at north end of water, which shows classic succession from open water through reed swamps to woodland carr.
□Access to Esthwaite Water restricted, but fine views from B5285 and Water Side Woods on east shore. OS 96 & 97: 96 36.
□*Bowness to Hawkshead* (National Park Walksheet No. W.3.) passes over Claife Heights (see 8) and includes taking the ferry across Lake Windermere.
□*National Park Information Centre*, (leaflets, nature trails, maps etc.) The main Square, Hawkshead. Open daily, Easter–September.
□*National Trust Information Centre*. (leaflets, maps), The Main Square, Hawkeshead. Open daily, Easter-October.

17 Fell Foot Park.
National Trust. Parkland at edge of Lake Windermere. Rhododendrons, ornamental trees and woodland. Views of reedbeds and willow carr at foot of lake. Many ducks. Information Centre, cafe, picnic area.
□Newby Bridge, Near Ulverston (Tel: Newby Bridge 273). Park open all year; Information Centre open daily, Easter–October. 10½ miles/ 17 km north-east of Ulverston. Turn off A590 onto A592 at Newby Bridge. OS 96 & 97: 381 869.

18 Fitzpark Museum
Good collection of typical Lakeland birds such as Raven, Buzzard and Peregrine. Mammals include Pine Marten, Red Squirrel, Otter and Badger. Moth and butterfly collection. Geological exhibits and raised relief map of Lake District made in 1834.
□Station Road, Keswick (Tel Keswick 73263). Open April–October, daily except Sunday.

19 Friars Crag

Nature Walk. National Trust and Cumbria Naturalists' Trust. Walk along north-east shore of Derwent Water through woodland. Plants include Wood Sorrel, Bluebell and Foxglove. Great Spotted Woodpecker, tits and warblers in woods, with Coot, Tufted Duck, Pochard, Goldeneye and Cormorant on lake; Heron and Common Sandpiper along shore. Rare fish, the Vendace, in lake. Leaflet available from National Trust Information Centres; route for wheelchairs.

□Just south of Keswick on B5289, park in Lakeside car park. OS 89: 265 228.

20 Graythwaite Hall Gardens

Formal gardens with shrubs including Rhododendrons and Azaleas.

□Newby Bridge, Near Ulverston (Tel: Newby Bridge 31248). Open daily, April–June. 12½ miles/20 km north-east of Ulverston. Turn north off A590 at Newby Bridge onto unclassified road to Far Sawry, along west side of Lake Windermere. OS 96 & 97: 371 913.

21 Grizedale Forest

Forestry Commission. Large area lying between Lake Windermere and Coniston Water with conifer plantations and some broadleaved and mixed woodlands. Birds include Buzzard, Raven, Black Grouse, Woodcock, Pied Flycatcher, Redstart, Treecreeper, Goldcrest, Green and Great Spotted Woodpeckers and Crossbill. Red and Roe Deer, Fox, Badger and Red Squirrel. Adder, Grass Snake and Common Lizard. Wildlife observation hides for hire. Visitor Centre and Information Room with interpretative displays explaining geology, soils, land use, wildlife and modern forestry; publications, leaflets, forest maps.

□Information Centre, Grizedale, Ambleside (Tel: Satterthwaite 272 & 273) Visitor Centre open daily, all year; Information Room open daily, Easter-October. OS 96 & 97: 336 943.

□*Millwood Forest Trail.* Along beck, through old Oak, Douglas Fir and Norway Spruce forest, passing wildlife conservation area. Leaflet. Starts near Visitor Centre.

□*Silurian Way.* Way-marked, long-distance walk through plantations of Oak, Larch, Spruce and Pine. Leaflet. Starts at Visitor Centre.

□*Bogle Crag Walks.* Three way-marked walks through Lakeland forest. Start at Bogle Crag picnic site, ½ mile/1 km south of Visitor Centre on Hawkshead to Satterthwaite road. OS 96 & 97: 337 933.

□*Spruce Knott Observation Hide.* Red and Roe Deer, woodland birds and wildfowl on Woodmoss tarn. Permit only; apply Chief Forester, Forest Office, Grizedale, Hawkshead Near Ambleside (Tel: Satterthwaite 272).

22 Hawkshead Courthouse

National Trust. Museum of local rural life; forestry exhibits.

□Open Easter and May–October, daily except Monday (open Bank Holidays), afternoons only. 5 miles/8 km south of Ambleside on B5286 at junction with B5285. OS 96 & 97: 349 987.

23 Haybridge Nature Reserve and Deer Museum

Reserve includes part of Rusland Moss, as well as woodland, open fell, farmland, tidal river, stream and pond. Native deer and other mammals. Museum contains exhibits of deer and collections of moths, butterflies and birds. Lecture rooms, hides, picnic area.

□Open daily by appointment only; apply to Warden, Deer Museum, Low Hay Bridge, Bouth-by-Ulverston (Tel: Greenodd 412). 3 miles/5 km north of Haverthwaite on unclassified road via Bouth. OS 96 & 97: 337 879.

24 Holehird

Gardens. Many exotic trees such as Eucalyptus, Mulberry, Tree of Heaven and Tulip Tree. Rhododendrons and Azaleas, collection of recently planted Camellias and rare ferns. Wild flowers include Violets, Wood Anemone and Lords and Ladies. Guide booklet. Conducted tours available if arranged in advance.

□Patterdale Road, Windermere. Open daily, all year. ¾ mile/1 km north of Windermere, east off A592. OS 90: 410 007.

25 Johnny's Wood
Woodland walk. National Trust and Cumbria Naturalists' Trust. Passes over open fell and through Oak and Ash woods. Sundew, Bog Asphodel, Marsh Pennywort, Lousewort and Marsh Orchid grow in damp area; Dog's Mercury, Wood Sorrel, Dog Violet and various ferns in wood. Birds include Willow Warbler, Redstart, Common Sandpiper and Dipper; occasionally Buzzard. Red Squirrel also found. Leaflet available from National Trust Information Centres and Cumbria Naturalists' Trust, Rydal Road, Ambleside (Tel: Ambleside 2476).
□8 miles/ 13 km south of Keswick on B5289 to Seatoller. OS 90: 254 139.

26 Launchy Ghyll
Forest trail. North West Water Authority. Norway Spruce and Scots Pine plantation, with Birch, Hazel, Oak and Rowan growing along the edges. Mosses and ferns. Woodland birds. Red and Roe Deer and Red Squirrel. Leaflet available at beginning of trail or from Public Information Unit, North West Water Authority, Dawson House, Great Sankey, Warrington (Tel: Penketh 4321).
□6 miles/10 km south of Keswick, on west side of Thirlmere, take 'scenic road' west off A591. OS 90: 309 158.

27 Lingholm
Formal and woodland gardens overlooking Derwent Water. Large collection of Rhododendrons and other interesting shrubs and trees. Leaflet available. Good for woodland birds.
□Portinscale, Keswick (Tel: Keswick 72003). Open daily excluding Sunday, April–October. 2 miles/3 km south-west of Keswick, turn south off A66 for Portinscale, turn off Grange road 1 mile/1.5 km south of Portinscale. OS 89: 253 222.

28 Lowther Wildlife Park
130 acres/53 ha of parkland with Red, Fallow and Sika Deer, and Old English Longhorn Cattle. Woodland pens with Boar and Wolves; collection of British mammals including Wild Cat, Fox, Badger and Polecat. Decoy pond with Red-crested Pochard, Pintail, Tufted Duck, Shoveler, Gadwall and Barnacle and Pink-footed Geese, Snowy, Eagle and Tawny Owls and free-flying Macaws. Guide book, leaflets, shop, cafe, picnic area.
□Lowther, Penrith (Tel: Hackthorpe 523). Open daily, Easter–October. 4 miles/6.5 km south of Penrith, off A6. OS 90: 533 225.

29 Muncaster Castle and Bird Garden
Formal gardens and parkland with Rhododendrons and Azaleas. Tropical bird collection includes parrots, cardinals, a number of rare pheasants, cranes and ibises. Mammals include wallabies and Himalayan Bear. Nature trail.
□Ravenglass (Tel: Ravenglass 614). Open Easter–September; gardens, from noon daily excluding Friday; castle, Tuesday, Wednesday, Thursday and Sunday afternoons. OS 96: 103 964.

30 Nether Wasdale
Nature trail. Cumbria Naturalists' Trust. Mixed woodland at southern end of Wast Water. Flowers include those associated with poor acid soil; Tormentil, Bilberry and Harebell, with Bog Asphodel, Sundew and Butterwort in wetter areas; also Wood Sorrel and Wood Sage. Birds include Great Spotted and Green Woodpeckers, Pied Flycatcher. Redstart and Wood Warbler; Red-breasted Merganser on lake and Common Sandpiper, Dipper and Grey Wagtail along river; occasionally Buzzard, Raven and Peregrine. Nature trail leaflet available from Cumbria Naturalists' Trust, Rydal Road, Ambleside (Tel: Ambleside 2476).
□7 miles/11 km north east of Ravenglass, turn east off A595 to Santon Bridge, then take road north for Strands, at fork in road continue right. Park at shore of Wast Water. OS 89: 146 047.

31 Rothay Valley and Loughrigg
Environmental walk. National Trust and Charlotte Mason College of Education. Passes beside a beck, through woodland and over open fell. Trees include Silver Birch, Bird Cherry and Crab Apple. Typical plants of poor ground: Tormentil, Heath

Bedstraw, Bilberry, Wood Sorrel, Foxglove and Butterwort. Interesting ferns such as Parsley Fern and Maidenhair Spleenwort. Woodland birds, Dippers and Common Sandpipers along beck. Leaflet available from National Trust Information Centres.
□Walk starts at Bridge House, Ambleside OS 90: 370 043.

32 Roudsea Wood National Nature Reserve
Nature Conservancy Council. A varied woodland as part lies over Carboniferous Limestone and part over more acidic rock. Trees include Sessile Oak, Ash, Yew, Blackthorn, Hazel and Spindle. Many ferns, also Herb Paris, Lily of the Valley and Yellow Sedge. Good for woodland birds. Roe Deer and Badger. Leaflet available. Limited parking.
□Permit required away from rights of way; apply to Regional Officer, Nature Conservancy Council, Blackwell, Bowness-on-Windermere (Tel: Windermere 5286). Reserve lies 10 miles/16 km west of Grange-over-Sands, on north-east side of Leven Estuary. Turn south off A590 to Haverthwaite, after crossing River Leven track leads down to reserve. OS 96 & 97: 330 825.

33 Rusland Hall
Garden landscaped by Capability Brown; good specimen trees. White Peacocks.
□Newby Bridge (Tel: Satterthwaite 276). Open daily, April–September. 3 miles/5 km north of Newby Bridge on Satterthwaite road. OS 96 & 97: 342 888.

34 Rydal Mount
Family home of William Wordsworth. Garden landscaped by poet, overlooking Windermere and Rydal Water; woodland and variety of trees. In spring the daffodils immortalised by Wordsworth can be seen in Dora's field nearby.
□Rydal (Tel: Ambleside 3002). Open daily, March–mid-January. 1½ miles/2 km north of Ambleside. OS 90: 364 063.

35 Stagshaw
National Trust. Woodland garden on a slope overlooking Lake Windermere. Unique collection of Rhododendrons, Azaleas, Camellias and spring bulbs.
□Open daily, all year. ½ mile/1 km south of Ambleside on A591. OS 90: 38 02.

36 Stanley Ghyll
Nature trail. Passes through ravine with Oak, Sycamore, Hazel, Rowan and a number of conifers. Bilberry, Wood Sage and Heath Bedstraw grow along the grassy banks; some interesting mosses and liverworts in damper areas. Leaflet. (see also 15).
□Trail starts from Dalegarth Station at top of Ravenglass and Eskdale Railway. OS 89: 173 007.

37 Swirls
Forest trail. North West Water Authority. Many different species of conifer trees including Douglas Fir, Noble Fir, Western Hemlock and Japanese and European Larch. Red Squirrel. Leaflet available at beginning of trail or from Public Information Unit, North West Water Authority, Dawson House, Great Sankey, Warrington (Tel: Penketh 4321).
□6 miles/ 10 km south of Keswick, east side of Thirlmere on A591. OS 90: 316 168.

38 Tarn Hows
National Trust. Small upland lake, created from three natural tarns, surrounded by coniferous forest. Good views. Wetland plants. Red-breasted Merganser, Greylag Goose, Common Sandpiper and Tree Pipit. Nature trail with leaflet.
□*Three walks in Skelwith Bridge and Tarn Hows area* (National Park Walksheet No. W.8.): around tarn and onto fells beyond; around Elterwater, good for breeding wildfowl and wintering swans; through a variety of habitats with magnificent views of Langdale Pikes.
□Tarn Hows is 2 miles/3 km north of Coniston, north off B5285 at Hawkshead Hill. OS 96 & 97: 326 995.

39 Thornthwaite Forest
Forestry Commission. Mature plantations of Sitka Spruce on high ground with Larch, Douglas Fir and Red Cedar on low ground. Roe Deer, Red Squirrel and rare Pine

Marten. Birds include Buzzard and Sparrowhawk. Visitor Centre with displays and tape-slide presentations telling story of Man's impact on the fells and modern forestry; leaflets.

□Visitor Centre open daily, Easter–October. North off B5292 between High Lorton and Braithwaite at Whinlatter Pass. OS 89: 208 245.

□*Comb Trail* Good views of Bassenthwaite and Derwent Water. Starts at Visitor Centre.

□*Noble Knott Walks*. Series of waymarked walks through old Oaks, young Silver and Douglas Firs, Larch and Spruce. Starts 1 mile/1.5 km east of Visitor Centre. OS 89: 223 244.

40 Ullswater

Lake known for its twisting shoreline; area has great variety of views. Many exotic trees such as Copper Beech, Wellingtonias and a variety of Oaks. Extensive Juniper scrub on Birk Fell on south-east shore. Biggest waterfall in Lake District, Aira Force.

□*Three walks in the Ullswater area* (National Park Walksheet No. W.9.): around Aira Force; Grizedale Beck; southern shore of Ullswater from Patterdale to Howton.

□*National Park Information Centres* (leaflets, displays, etc.) open daily Easter–September. Beckside Car Park, Glenridding, OS 90: 385 169 and Eusemere Lodge Car Park, Pooley Bridge, OS 90: 470 243.

41 Whitbarrow

Limestone pavement, escarpment, grassland, woodland, cliffs and scree. Plants include Blue Moorgrass, Lesser Meadowrue and several ferns. For more detailed description of plants of limestone areas see page 17. Good for birds with Buzzard, Woodcock, Nightjar, Raven and both Great Spotted and Green Woodpeckers. Fox, Roe and Red Deer in woods. Keep to the public rights of way as this is private land.

□7 miles/11 km north of Grange-over-Sands, turn north off A590 at the Derby Arms, just before entrance of Witherslack Hall follow signed footpath to Lords Seat, highest part of escarpment. OS 97: 442 871.

42 White Moss Common

Nature walk. National Trust and Cumbria Naturalists' Trust. Typical Lake District country – woodland, open fell and lake shores of Rydal Water and Grasmere. Cotton Grass, Scabious, Spearwort, Bogbean, Bog Myrtle, Yellow Pimpernel, Creeping Buttercup, Common Stitchwort and Marsh Violet all occur. Woodpeckers, Treecreeper and Pied Flycatcher. Leaflet available from National Trust Information Centres.

□2 miles/ 3 km north-west of Ambleside on A591. Park in old White Moss Quarry or on White Moss Common. OS 90: 348 065.

43 Windermere

Largest lake, 10 miles/16 km long by 1 mile/1.5 km wide. Well wooded shores with tits and warblers nesting. Waterbirds include Tufted Duck, Great Crested Grebe, Teal, Mallard, Pochard, Shelduck, Red-breasted Merganser, Goosander, Goldeneye and Cormorant; Common Sandpiper and Dipper along shore. Char is one of species of fish found in lake.

□*Three walks around Windermere and Bowness.* (National Park Walksheet No. W. 10.): lake shore and Claife Heights (see 8); Orrest Head; lake shore and Adelaide Hill.

□*National Park Information Centre* (leaflets, displays etc.) Bowness Bay, Bowness-on-Windermere. Open daily Easter–September.

Lancashire

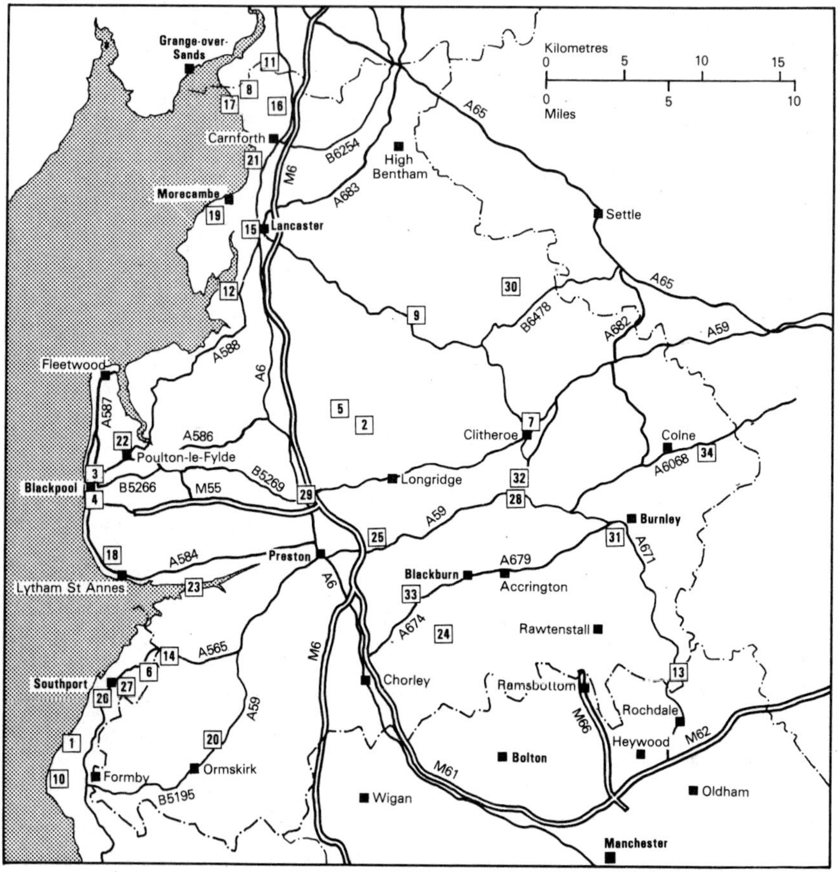

1 Ainsdale Sand Dunes National Nature Reserve (Merseyside)
Nature Conservancy Council. Fourth largest sand dune system in Britain. 400 species of plants have been identified. Dune Helleborine and local varieties of Round-leaved Wintergreen and Grass of Parnassus are of particular interest because they are confined to this coast. Other species include Sea Spurge, Rest-harrow, Dewberry, Common Centaury, Yellow-wort, Carline Thistle, Evening Primrose, Marsh Helleborine, Yellow Iris and Early Marsh Orchid; reeds and many kinds of rushes and sedges; Willow Warbler, Whitethroat, Linnet, Reed Bunting, waders and gulls; Redwing and Fieldfares in winter. Rabbit, Hare, Fox and Red Squirrel; reptiles well represented with Common and Sand Lizard, Frog, Common Toad, Common Newt and Natterjack Toad. Booklet available.

☐ Permit required away from public rights of way and concessionary footpaths; apply to Regional Officer, Nature Conservancy Council, Blackwell, Bowness-on-Windermere, Cumbria (Tel: Windermere 5286). 2 miles/3 km north of Formby, west of A565. Park at Freshfield Station and follow Montagu Road and then Fisherman's Footpath which leads to reserve. OS 108: 287 103.

2 Beacon Fell Country Park
Lancashire County Council. Mixed woodland with open areas of heather and rough grazing. Bilberry, Cotton Grass and Heath Bedstraw. Woodland birds with Red Grouse, Lapwing and Curlew on moor. Painted Lady, Small Copper and Green-veined White butterflies. Hare, Fox, Weasel, Stoat and Hedgehog. Information Centre, booklet, forest walks.
□Park open throughout year, Information Centre open at weekends, and most days of the week, March–September. 8 miles/13 km north of Preston, signposted from Longridge, Broughton (on A6, 3½ miles/ 6 km north of Preston) and Brock Bridge (on A6, 14 miles/22.5 km south of Lancaster). OS 102: 568 428.

3 Blackpool Tower Aquarium
One of the best aquariums in the country, especially noted for its coral fish. Over 200 species of fish. Also tropical aviary, butterfly garden and tropical garden.
□The Promenade, Blackpool (Tel: Blackpool 25252). Open daily, May–October.

4 Blackpool Zoo
Large collection of mammals from all parts of the world including Tiger, Elephant, Rhinoceros, Orangutan, and Sea-lions. Lectures and films organised for school parties. Guide book and leaflets; shop, cafe and picnic sites.
□East Park Drive, Blackpool (Tel: Blackpool 65027). Open daily all year excluding Christmas Day

5 Brock Valley
Mixed woodland with stream. Plants include Policeman's Helmet, Wild Garlic, Yellow Iris, Common Butterbur, Golden Saxifrage, Sweet Cecily and Lesser Reedmace. Good variety of woodland birds with Dipper, Common Sandpiper and Grey Wagtail along stream. Guide from Publications Officer, Lancashire Naturalists' Trust, 134 Fylde Road, Southport. (Tel: Southport 24110).
□10 miles/16 km north of Preston, turn east off A6 1 mile/1.5 km north of Bilsbarrow, onto unclassified road via Claughton to Brock Mill. OS 102: 549 431.

6 Churchtown Botanic Gardens Museum
Exhibits include natural history, local geology, displays on the local shrimping industry and the Ainsdale National Nature Reserve (see 1).
□Churchtown, Southport (Tel: Southport 27547). Open Tuesday – Saturday, all year.

7 Clitheroe Castle Museum
Important collection of Carboniferous fossils. Magnificent views over Ribble Valley from grounds. Suitable for wheelchairs.
□(Tel: Clitheroe 24635). Open Tuesday, Thursday, Saturday and Sunday, Easter–September.

8 Eaves Wood
Woodland walk. National Trust and Lancashire Naturalists' Trust. Open woodland on limestone hillside with outcrops of limestone pavement. Plants include lime-loving species such as Dropwort, Carline Thistle, Thyme and Lily of the Valley Woodland birds such as Great Spotted Woodpecker and Woodcock. Wood Ants. Leaflet available from National Trust Information Centres.
□4 miles/6.5 km north of Carnforth. Take road north out of Silverdale, past chapel and park in car park ½ mile/1 km further on. Entrance to wood on north side of car park. OS 97: 467 762

9 Forest of Bowland
Area of Outstanding Natural Beauty. Wild moorland fells offer some of the roughest and most remote walking in Lancashire. Good area for birds such as Merlin, Hen Harrier, Short-eared Owl and Ring Ouzel, with Black Grouse on the moorland edges. (See also 30).
□Leaflet available on access areas from County Estates Surveyor, Winckley House, Winckley Square, Preston, or the Head Ranger (Tel: Forton 791075). Main areas: Clougha, car parking at Jubilee Tower OS 102: 542 574; Birkbank OS 97: 526 604; Little Cragg OS 97: 546 618; Fairsnape, Saddle Fell and Wolf Fell, parking at Chipping Village OS 102 & 103: 622 433; Beacon Fell Country Park (see 2).

10 Formby Sands (Merseyside)
National Trust. Sand dunes and shore, also some coniferous woodland and areas of scrub. Similar flora to Ainsdale National Nature Reserve which it adjoins. Good for small migrants and waders; occasional skuas and shearwaters. Nature trail with guide available from National Trust Regional Office, Attingham Park, Shrewsbury, Salop (Tel Upton Magna 202 & 649) or from Publications Officer, Lancashire Naturalists' Trust, 134 Fylde Road, Southport.
□2 miles/3 km west of Formby, park by Freshfield Station or take road by station west towards sea and park just before disused lighthouse. OS 108: 275 075.

11 Gait Barrows National Nature Reserve
Nature Conservancy Council. One of the best examples of limestone pavement in country. Also deciduous scrub and woodland, with Willow and Alder carr. Deadly Nightshade, Bloody Cranesbill, Tutsan, Dark-Red Helleborine, Mountain St John's Wort, and Lily of the Valley all occur. Variety of woodland birds. Rare molluscs and insects.
□Permit required away from footpaths; apply to Regional Officer, North-West Regional Office, Nature Conservancy Council, Blackwell, Bowness-on-Windermere. Reserve is 5 miles/8 km north of Carnforth, turn west off A6 at Beetham onto unclassified road to Silverdale. Limited parking. OS 97: 478 767.

12 Glasson Dock and Lune Estuary
Nature trail. Circular footpath passing by area of saltmarshes and returning along canal and disused railway track. Waders such as Redshank and Lapwing; also Shelduck and Wigeon. Thrift on shore, Kidney Vetch and Bird's Foot Trefoil on railway. Flowers by canal include Sweet Flag, Yellow Iris and Great Willowherb. Guide available from Publications Officer, Lancashire Naturalists' Trust, 134 Flyde Road, Southport.
□4 miles/6.5 km south of Lancaster on A588, park at Conder Green. OS 102: 45 56.

13 Healey Dell Local Nature Reserve
Rochdale Metropolitan Borough Council and Rossendale Borough Council. Steep wooded valley formed by River Spodden. Disused railway, remains of old water-driven textile mill and Victorian viaduct. Rich flora; Giant Bellflower, Crowberry, Skullcap, Sweet Woodruff, Golden Rod, Bog Asphodel, Sneezewort, Broadleaved Hellborine and various Marsh Orchids; introduced Pink Purslane is well established in the area. Birds include Woodcock, Great Spotted Woodpecker, Tawny Owl, Grey Wagtail and Twite. Nature trail, booklets and trail guide available from Recreation Department, Rochdale Metropolitan Borough Council, Town Hall, Rochdale (Tel: Rochdale 47474), or from Publications Officer, Lancashire Naturalists' Trust. Please keep to public rights of way as much of the land is private.
□2 miles/3 km north of Rochdale off A671 just through village of Healey near junction with B6377. OS 109: 880 159.

14 Hesketh Park
Originally sand hills on which a wide variety of trees were planted. Park now comprises ornamental gardens, a lake with some wildfowl, a conservatory and aviaries where birds such as Guinea Fowl, Peacock and parrots may be seen.
□Southport (Tel: Southport 33963). Open daily, all year. North-east side of Southport, east of A565.

15 Hornsea Pottery
Pottery set in parkland with a Rare Breeds Survival Unit. Collection of domestic animals some of which were in danger of extinction: White Park and and Highland Cattle, Manx and Herdwick Sheep. Shops, cafe and picnic facilities.
□Wyresdale Road, Lancaster (Tel: Lancaster 68444). Open daily, all year.

16 Leighton Hall
Extensive grounds. Collection of birds of prey. Flying displays every afternoon, weather permitting. Natural history leaflet available.
□Yealand Conyers, Near Carnforth (Tel: Carnforth 2729) Open Tuesday–Friday

and Sundays, May–September, afternoons only. (Hall open Wednesday and Sunday). 3 miles/5 km north of Carnforth off A6. OS 97: 497 745.

17 Leighton Moss

Nature reserve. RSPB. Reedbed with open pools, scrub and woodland. Interesting for plants such as Bulrush and Water Plantain, but best known for its birds. Bittern, Bearded Tit, Reed and Sedge Warblers and Water Rail being just a few of its breeding birds. Ducks include Shoveler, Teal, Pintail, Wigeon and Garganey. Good for wading birds including Green and Wood Sandpipers, while some of the rarer species recorded include Purple Heron, Black Tern, Marsh Harrier and Osprey. Otters regularly seen. Good for insects including a number of less common moths. Interpretative Centre, leaflets. Public hide on causeway always open.

□Reserve open Saturday, Sunday, Wednesday and Thursday, April–September, please report to Interpretative Centre on arrival.To visit the reserve in winter contact Warden, Myers Farmhouse, Silverdale, Carnforth. ½ mile/1 km east of Silverdale. OS 97: 478 751.

18 Lytham St Annes

Local nature reserve. Fylde Borough Council. Dunes and slacks. Plants include Sea Buckthorn, Round-leaved Wintergreen, Kidney Vetch, Rest-Harrow, Carline Thistle, Dewberry, Yellow-wort and Early Marsh Orchid. Common birds and good selection of butterflies and moths. Booklet available from Parks Department Office, 7 St Georges Road, Lytham St Annes (Tel: Lytham St Annes 724141).

□Between Lytham St Annes and Blackpool, on inland side of A584, near Pontins Holiday Camp. OS 102: 310 306.

19 Marineland Oceanarium and Aquarium

Outdoor pools with dolphins and Sea-lions which give performances from May–September. Penguins. Indoor collection includes over 200 species of fish from all over the world; also reptiles such as turtles and alligators. Guide book, leaflets.

□Stone Jetty, Central Promenade, Morecambe (Tel: Morecambe 414727). Open daily Easter–October.

20 Martin Mere

Wildfowl Trust Centre and Site of Special Scientific Interest. 45 acres/18 ha consists of pens, lakes and wildfowl gardens which house over 100 species of ducks, geese and swans from all parts of the world. Also 300 acres/121ha of wetland with 20 acre lake providing an important wild habitat for waders and wildfowl. These include Pink-footed and White-fronted Geese, Whooper and Bewick's Swans, Pintail, Tufted Duck, Shoveler, Gadwall and Wigeon. Also Ruff, Black-tailed Godwit, Little Ringed Plover and Redshank. Hen Harrier, Merlin and Peregrine Falcon may be seen in winter. Good all year round but arrival of the winter wildfowl is particularly interesting. Bird hides, unique visitor centre incorporating educational complex, cinema, lecture hall with exhibitions. Guided tours and field studies by arrangement, guide book, leaflets, shop, cafe, picnic areas.

□Burscough, Near Ormskirk (Tel: Burscough 895181). Open daily excluding Christmas Eve and Christmas Day. 10 miles/16 km east of Southport, signposted from Burscough Bridge Station. OS 108: 425 141.

21 Morecambe Bay

Large area of intertidal sand and mud, with saltmarshes, creeks and grazing marshes. Rich flora, just a few species being Sea Milkwort, Thrift, Sea Aster, Sea Rocket, Sea Beet and Sea Lavender. Holds biggest population of wintering waders in Britain. These include Dunlin, Redshank, Knot, Sanderling, Ringed Plover, Oystercatcher, Bar-tailed Godwit, Turnstone and Curlew. Ducks include Goldeneye, Red-breasted Merganser, Goosander, Scaup, Wigeon, Shelduck; also Greylag and Pink-footed Geese. Many species of gulls and several terns; occasionally skuas.

□Good views from Hest Bank signal box (OS 97: 467 666) and from several of the roads that border the bay. On lower tides a walk along the shoreline from the north end of Morecambe Promenade gives good views; beware of dangerous channels and quicksands on foreshore.

22 Poulton-le-Fylde Urban Trail

Lancashire Naturalists' Trust. Passes through town and park. Leaflet describing trees, flowers and birds that can be seen, available from 134 Fylde Road, Southport (Tel: Southport 24110).

□Trail begins in Breck Road, Poulton-le-Fylde (north-east of Blackpool).

23 Ribble Estuary

Extensive sandflats and saltmarsh. The west Lancashire coast is a good area in Britain for the Pink-footed Goose, large numbers of which can be seen along the Ribble estuary in winter. Also large numbers of wintering waders with Dunlin and Knot particularly numerous. Breeding birds include Redshank, Lapwing, Oystercatcher, Skylark, Black-headed Gull and Common Tern.

□Estuary has footpaths on either bank. From south follow unclassified road from Crossens to Hundred End and Hesketh Bank. On north side footpath can be joined at Freckleton on A568, OS 102: 434 284.

24 Roddlesworth

Nature trail. Woodland and moorland with marsh and boggy areas near river. Oak, Beech and Bird Cherry, with ground flora of Golden Rod, Adder's Tongue Fern, Common St John's Wort, Marsh Cinquefoil, Water Dropwort, Melancholy Thistle, Figwort and several species of fern. Woodcock, Goldcrest, Treecreeper, Kingfisher, Grey Wagtail, Redstart, Redpoll and Siskin are just a few of birds to be seen. Trail booklet from Mr S. Fielding, 2 Engine Brow, Tockholes, Darwen or from Lancashire Naturalists' Trust. Please keep to public footpath as adjacent land is private.

□4 miles/6.5 km south of Blackburn, east off A 675. Park next to Royal Arms Hotel. OS 103: 664 216

25 Salmesbury Hall and Nature Reserve

Fourteenth-century moated manor house with formal gardens. Across the road is a nature reserve managed by the Council for the Protection of Rural England; leaflet available from the Council's offices adjacent to the Hall. Reserve is an old Japanese water garden that has been allowed to return to a wild state. Oak, Ash, Beech, Birch and Alder, with ornamental species such as Cherry, Rhododendrons and Laburnum. Flowers include Wood Anemone, Bluebell and Wood Sorrel, with Yellow Iris and Bulrush in wetter areas. Large number of woodland birds including several species of warbler, Marsh and Long-tailed Tits. Grey Squirrels.

□Tel: Mellor 2229 (Hall) or 3360 (CPRE). Open daily except Monday; closed mid-December–mid-January. Access to reserve at all times. 4 miles/6.5 km east of Preston, off A677. OS 102 & 103: 626 306.

26 Southport Aquarium

About fifty species of fish, mainly freshwater. Reptiles include snakes, small crocodiles, iguanas, lizards and terrapins. Also Axolotl and frogs.

□Marine Parade (Tel: Southport 32553). Open daily, Easter–September.

27 Southport Zoo

Set in attractive grounds with tropical plants and flower gardens. Mammals include Leopard, Lynx, Malayan Small-clawed Otter, Wallabies and the biggest collection of breeding Mandrills in Europe. Reptiles include alligators, snakes, lizards, Giant Seychelles Tortoise; aquarium with tropical and coldwater fish. Assorted aviaries house flamingoes, Giant Hornbill, owls and a good collection of parrots. Guide book, shop, and cafe. Lectures may be arranged for groups and school parties. Suitable for wheelchairs.

□Princes Park (Tel: Southport 38102). Open daily excluding Christmas Day.

28 Spring Wood

Lancashire County Council. Mixed woodland of Birch, Sycamore, Alder, Ash, Scots Pine, Larch, Beech and Rowan. Flowers include Wood Anemone, Wood Sorrel, Bluebell, Yellow Iris and Wild Garlic. Woodland birds, especially tits and warblers. Nature trail; leaflet available

from County Estates Surveyor, Winckley House, Winckley Square, Preston, or from Lancashire Naturalist's Trust. Picnic area.
□3½ miles/6 km south of Clitheroe, on A671 at junction with Whalley easterly by-pass. OS 103: 742 363.

29 Squire Anderton's Wood
Old mixed woodland with stream. Wild Garlic, Common Bistort, Wood Anemone, Woodruff and Lords and Ladies. Good for woodland birds with several species of tits and warblers, also Treecreeper and Goldcrest. Nature trail; leaflet available from Publications Officer, Lancashire Naturalists' Trust, 134 Fylde Road, Southport (Tel: Southport 24110)
□3 miles/5 km north of Preston, leave M55 at junction 1, north for Broughton, turn almost immediately right for Haighton Top, park under bridge of M6. OS 102: 560 337.

30 Stocks Reservoir
North West Water Authority. Set in the Forest of Bowland (see 9). Excellent birdwatching area. Many birds of prey including Buzzard and several species of owls. Waders include Curlew, Lapwing, Snipe and Redshank. Wide variety of wildfowl, especially in winter. Many passage migrants may be seen in autumn.
□Permit required for most of the surrounding area; apply to Divisional Manager, Ribble Division, Pennine House, Stanley Street, Preston. Open access with good views from unclassified road on east side of reservoir. 10 miles/16 km north of Clitheroe, turning north off B6478. OS 103: 73 56.

31 Towneley Hall Museum
Museum exhibits include archeology and natural history. Formal gardens and parkland with a nature trail. Nature centre with displays of local natural history; facilities for school field studies. Leaflet available on site.
□Burnley (Tel: Burnley 24213). Open Monday–Friday and Sunday afternoons, all year.

32 Whalley Abbey
Gardens with some woodland running down to the River Calder. Birds include Jackdaw, Rook, Spotted Flycatcher and several species of tits. Beech mast (fruit) attacts Brambling and Chaffinch. Grey Herons may be seen by the river.
□(Tel: Whalley 2268). Open daily, all year. 7 miles/11 km north east of Preston. OS 103: 73 36.

33 Witton Country Park
Blackburn Borough Council. 480 acres/194 ha of farmland and parkland with woodland, mainly deciduous, some areas of heath, rough grassland and wetland. Wide variety of plants and birds. Nature trails and tree trail. Visitor Centre with natural history exhibits.
□Visitor Centre open Thursday–Saturday, afternoons only, all day Sundays and Bank Holidays. Main entrance on A674, 1 mile/1.5 km west of Blackburn, OS 103: 663 270.

34 Wycoller Country Park
Lancashire County Council. Heather moor and grassland. Nature trail; leaflet available from the Ranger on duty at weekends and Bank Holidays, or from County Estates Surveyor, Winckley House, Winckley Square, Preston.
□3 miles/5 km east of Colne on unclassified road east off B6250. OS 103: 926 395.

Conservation

Britain still offers a variety of habitats rich in wildlife, and areas of wild and beautiful countryside; but these areas are threatened as more land is taken up by industry, housing and agriculture.

When hedgerows are removed and woodlands are cleared, wetlands drained, heaths replaced by forestry plantations, and trees felled indiscriminately, vital habitats are destroyed. The aim of wildlife conservation is to preserve existing habitats and manage them so as to ensure that the species dependent upon these habitats survive.

In Britain the official organization for the conservation of wildlife is the Nature Conservancy Council. They seek to inform farmers, planners and industrialists about environmental problems and to gain their co-operation in caring for the environment. The Council also protects important habitats by setting aside certain areas as nature reserves.

The ultimate responsibility for the survival of our wildlife lies with everyone, if the variety of countryside and wildlife is to remain and be enjoyed by future generations. The Countryside Commission has drawn up guidelines for visitors to the countryside. The main points are listed below.

The Country Code

Guard against all risk of fire.
Fasten all gates.
Keep dogs under proper control.
Keep to the paths across farm land.
Avoid damaging fences, hedges, walls.
Leave no litter.
Safeguard water supplies.
Protect wildlife, wild plants and trees.
Go carefully on country roads.
Respect the life of the countryside.

● *The Conservation of Wild Creatures and Wild Plants Act* makes it illegal to pick certain plants which are so rare as to be endangered, and to uproot *any wild plant* without the landowner's permission.

● *The Bird Protection Act* makes it illegal to take the eggs or disturb any wild bird at its nest.

Conservation in Cumbria and Lancashire

Visitor pressure is a problem in the region: peak periods are Bank Holidays and some of these coincide with the main nesting and flowering periods for many birds and plants. Boating on rivers and lakes and fishing and picnicking along the shores result in the destruction of vegetation and the disturbance of birds and mammals. Heavy public pressure along the coast has also meant the loss of many fine sites, causing some tern colonies to move or disappear. Dune areas are especially vulnerable, as they are easily eroded by trampling feet.

The mountains are eroded and alpine plants destroyed by more and more rock climbers using traditional routes and also establishing new ones. Skiing has damaged some fine areas, especially on the limestone grasslands of the Pennines, causing compaction of the soil and cutting up the turf during thaw periods.

As in other parts of Britain, changes in agricultural practice have taken their toll. Hedges have been removed, wet fields drained, ploughed and re-seeded and chemicals and fertilizers liberally used.

The Nature Conservancy Council and the County Naturalists' Trust have managed to protect some of the better areas and the Lake District Special Planning Board has recently drawn up a National Park Plan which gives additional attention to nature conservation. However, many problems still remain such as the removal of limestone pavement and other limestone for ornamental rock gardens. Although against the law, the use of poison baits is still prevalent and affects the numbers of Buzzards, Ravens and many other birds. Many fine broadleaved woodlands are still being cut down and replanted with alien conifers.

The two most frightening threats however are the extraction of more water from the lakes for the industrial cities of Northern England and the building of a barrage around Morecambe Bay or one of the other estuaries, which could have a disasterous effect on the huge wader populations to be found there.

Hill Safety

The weather on hills and mountains can change quickly, and it is always colder and generally windier at higher altitudes. Wind and rain on mountain tops can cause exhaustion and exposure. It is always advisable when going walking in hills and mountains to be well-prepared and be reasonably careful. Here are some guidelines:

- Don't be over-ambitious when planning walks, especially with children.
- Take note of weather forecasts and local information Notice Boards before setting off. Be prepared to change your route or turn bank if the weather turns bad.
- Leave word with someone before setting off of where you intend to walk and how long you expect to be out.
- Wear or take with you warm clothing, including windproof and waterproof outer clothing, and headgear and gloves. Wear boots rather than shoes and never wear smooth soles, especially not smooth-soled rubber boots.
- A rucksack leaves your hands free for scrambling up and down steeper slopes.

Carry the following items:
Good maps, preferably Ordnance Survey.
A survival bag or tent for shelter.
A compass: in misty conditions, using a compass may be the only means of finding your way back.
Energy-rich food such as chocolate and glucose sweets.
A basic first aid kit such as elastoplast, lint, antiseptic, crepe bandage.
An acurate watch, a torch and a whistle.

- Avoid crossing streams, except for very narrow, shallow ones. Avoid treading on scree or loose rock.
- In an emergency, six flashes of a torch or six blasts on a whistle is the signal that you need help.

Useful Addresses

Countryside Commission, John Dower House, Crescent Place, Cheltenham, Glos. Concerned with the development and improvement of facilities for enjoyment of countryside. *Regional Office for Northern England*, Warwick House, Grantham Road, Newcastle-upon-Tyne.

County Naturalists' Trusts. Concerned with nature conservation; manages nature reserves. *Cumbria*: Rydal Road, Ambleside. *Lancashire:* (publications) 134 Fylde Road, Southport, (membership enquiries) 6 Yewlands Avenue, Fulwood, Preston.

Forestry Commission, North West Regional Office, Dee Hills Park, Chester, Cheshire. Publishes guides to forest walks, nature trails and recreational facilities on their land. *Regional Office for North-West England*, Dee Hills Park, Chester, Cheshire.

Lake District National Park Information Service, Bank House, High Street, Windermere, Cumbria.

National Trust, 42 Queen Anne's Gate, London SW1. Publishes guide to Trust properties. *Regional Office for Cumbria and Lancashire*, Broadlands, Ambleside, Cumbria.

Nature Conservancy Council, 19/20 Belgrave Square, London SW1. Government body responsible for nature conservation throughout Britain. Safeguards sites and species and offers advice on conservation issues to all whose activity affects the countryside. Publishes guides on national nature reserves and series of pamphlets on conservation topics. *Regional Office for North-West England*, Blackwell, Bowness-on-Windermere, Windermere, Cumbria.

RSPB (Royal Society for the Protection of Birds), The Lodge, Sandy, Bedfordshire. Manages natures reserves and organises educational facilities. *Regional Office for Northern England*, E. Floor, Milburn House, Dean Street, Newcastle-upon-Tyne.

Tourist Boards: Cumbria: Ellerthwaite, Windermere. *Lancashire*: The Last Drop Village, Bromley Cross, Bolton.

Further Reading

The Lake District. W. H. Pearsall & W. Pennington (Collins 1973)
**Natural History of the Lake District*. G. A. K. Hervey & J. A. G. Barnes (Warne: 1970)
The Lake District National Park. Edited by the Countryside Commission (H.M.S.O. London: 1979)
The Naturalist in Lakeland. E. Hardy (David & Charles: 1973)
The Lake District. R. Millward & A. Robinson (Eyre & Spottiswoode: 1970)
**Cumbria*. R. Millward & A. Robinson (Macmillan: 1972)
Lakeland Geology. E. H. Shackleton (Dalesman: 1966)
The Geography of Lakeland. J. C. Barringer (Dalesman: 1976)
Mountains and Moorlands. W. H. Pearsall (Collins: 1950)
**Lakeland Natural History*. Ernest Blezard (Carlisle Natural History Society: 1946)
Upper Teesdale. Ed A. R. Clapham (Collins: 1978)
Cumbria Naturalists' Trust News Letter (published twice a year by the Cumbria Naturalists' Trust, Ambleside)
The Natural History of Grange over Sands Grange Natural History Society
The Natural History of Arnside and Silverdale (Youth Hostel Association)
A Vertebrate Fauna of Lakeland. H. A. Macpherson (1892 reprint Paul Minet: 1972)
Lakeland Mammals. W. R. Mitchell & Peter Delap (Dalesman: 1976)

Ornithology

**The Birds of Lakeland*. Ernest Blezard (Carlisle Natural History Society: 1946)
**Lakeland Ornithology*. Ernest Blezard (ed) (Carlisle Natural History Society: 1954)
Birdwatching in Lancashire. Eric Hardy (Dalesman: 1979)
**Birds of the Liverpool Area* Eric Hardy (Buncle & Co.: 1941)
Lakeland Birds. W. R. Mitchell & R. W. Robson (Dalesman: 1976)
Pennine Birds. W. R. Mitchell & R. W. Robson (Dalesman: 1973)
**The Birds of Lancashire*. Clifford Oakes (Oliver & Boyd: 1953)
**The Birds of the Lake Counties*. Ralph Stokoe (Carlisle Natural History Society: 1962)
Birds of Westmorland and the Northern Pennines. J. O. Wilson (Hutchinson: 1973)
The Birds of Morecambe Bay. John Wilson (Dalesman: 1976)
Birds in Cumbria including a county natural history report (published annually by the Association of Natural History Societies in Cumbria)

Flora

Flowering Plants and Ferns of Cumbria. Geoffrey Halliday (Occasional paper No 4, University of Lancaster: 1978)
**Travis's Flora of South Lancashire*. J. P. Savidge (ed) (Liverpool Botanical Society: 1963)
**Mountain Flora of Lakeland*.D. A. Ratcliffe (Proceeds of Botanical Society of the British Isles, vol 4: 1963)
The Flora of West Lancashire. J. A. Wheldon & Albert Wilson (1907; reprint E. P. Publishing 1978)
**Flora of Westmorland*. A Wilson (Arbroath: 1938)

General Field Guides

The Concise British Flora in Colour. W. Keble Martin (Ebury Press & Michael Joseph: 1969)
The Wild Flowers of Britain and Northern Europe. R. Fitter, A. Fitter & M. Blamey (Collins: 1974)
Grasses. C. E. Hubbard (Penguin: 1968)
Grasses, Ferns, Mosses and Lichens of Great Britain and Ireland. R. Phillips (Pan: 1980)
The Handbook of British Mammals. G. B. Corbett & H. N. Southern (Blackwell: 1977)
A Field Guide to the Insects of Britain and Northern Europe. M. Chinery (Collins: 1976)
British Butterflies. R. Goodden (David & Charles: 1978)
A Field Guide to the Birds of Britain and Europe. R. Peterson, G. Mountfort & P. A. D. Hollom (Collins: 1954)

*Book now out of print but may be obtainable from libraries.

Index

Page numbers in bold refer to illustrations. Place names appearing in "Places to Visit" are generally listed under the appropriate category (eg. nature reserves, museums, country parks).

Aaron's Rod, **58**
Adder, 15, **16**, 106, 108
Agrimony, Hemp, 21, **68**
Alder, 21, 25, **92**, **96**, 105, 116
Ambleside, 105
Anemone, Beadlet, **84**
Dahlia, **84**
Daisy, **84**
Hermit Crab, **84**
Snakelocks, **84**
Anemone, Wood, 10, **20**, **72**, 99, 108, 116, 117
Angelica, 101
Wild, 21, 27, 105
Apple, Crab, 21, 109
aquariums,
Blackpool Tower, 113
Marineland Oceanarium, 115
Southport, 116
Arrowgrass, Marsh, 13
Sea, 28
Ash, 20. 21. **92**, **96**, 100, 105, 109, 110, 116
Aspen, **93**, **96**
Asphodel, Bog, 14, **15**, 26, 109, 114
Aster, Sea, 28, **62**, 102, 115
Avens, Water, 10, 32
Wood, 20
aviaries,
Muncaster Castle and Bird Garden, 109
Hesketh Park, 114
Awlwort, 24
Azalea, 108, 109, 110

Badger, 23, 31, **54**, 105, 106, 107, 108, 109, 110
Barnacle, Acorn, **87**
Star, **87**
Barrow Docks, 99
Bass, 30
Bat, Daubenton's, 31
Pipistrelle, 31
Bearberry, 10
Bedstraw, Heath, **13**, 109, 110, 113
Northern, 102
Beech, Common, 21, **94**, **96** 107, 116
Copper, 111
Belle Isle, 105
Bellflower, Giant, 114
Betony, 99
Bilberry, 10, 13, 14, 17, 21, **67**, 109, 110, 113
Bindweed, Greater, **64**
Sea, 29, **65**
Birch, 14, 21, 22, 105, 109, 116
Silver, 20, **93**, **96**, 109
Bistort, **64**, 99, 117
Alpine, 12
Bittern, **27**, 115
Blackbird, 22, 31, **48**
Blackcap, **22**, **46**
Blackthorn, 20, 110
Bluebell, 20, **63**, 108, 116
Bog Rosemary, 26
Bogbean, 14, **15**, 102, 111
Borrowdale, 105
Borrowdale Volcanic Series, 7, 9
Bracken (see Fern)
Bramble, 21, **78**
Brambling, 31, 117
Brittle Star, Common, **87**
Small, **87**
Brockhole, 105
Brooklime, **63**
Broom, **59**
Byrony, White, **73**
Buckthorn, 20
Alder, 21
Sea, 115
Bugle, 21, **63**
Bugloss, Viper's, **62**
Bullfinch, 22, **51**
Bulrush, 115, 116
Bunting, Corn, 31, **52**
Reed, **52**, 101, 112
Snow, 12, 31
Burnet, Great, 26, 32
Bur-reed, 101
Branched, 27
Floating, 14
Butterbur, Common, 113
White, 99
Buttercup, Bulbous, **57**
Creeping, **57** 111
Butterfly,
Admiral, Red, **80**
Argus, Brown, 23
Scotch, 17
Blue, Common, 17, **81**
Brimstone, 23, **82**, 99
Brown, Meadow, **79**, 106
Wall, **79**
Copper, Small, **81**, 106, 113
Duke of Burgundy, 23
Fritillary, Dark Green, **23**
Pearl-bordered, Small, 17
Grayling, **79**
Hairstreak, Green, 23
Purple, 23
Heath, Large, 26, **27**
Small, 17, **79**
Mountain Ringlet, Small, 12, **13**
Orange Tip, 23, **81**
Painted Lady, **80**, 113
Peacock, **80**, 106
Skipper, Dingy, 23
Tortoiseshell, Small, **80**, 106
White, Green-veined, **82**, 113
White, Large, **81**
White, Small, **82**
Buttermere, 105
Butterwort, 13, 102, 109, 110
Buzzard, **10**, 12, 22, **37**, 99, 103, 105, 106, 107, 108, 109, 111, 118

Cabbage, Isle of Man, 29, 106
Campion, Bladder, **76**
Red, **68**
Sea, 10, 29, **76**, 102
White, **76**
canal, 27
Glasson Dock, 114
Lancaster-Kendal, 5, 6, 27, 101
carr, 21, 107, 114
Carrot, Wild, **74**
Cat, Wild, 99, 109
Cedar, 100
Red, 110
Celandine, Lesser, 20, **57**
Centaury, Common, **66**, 112
Seaside, 29, **30**
Chaffinch, 22, 31, **50**, 117
Char, 111
Cherry, 116
Bird, 22, 109, 116
Wild, 21, 99
Chestnut, Horse, **95**, **96**
Sweet, **95**, **96**
Chickweed, **76**
Chiffchaff, 22, **47**
Cinquefoil, Alpine, 12, 100
Creeping, **60**
Marsh, 116
Claife Shore and Claife Heights, 106
cliffs, 4, 5, 6, 28
Humphrey Head, 100
St Bee's Head, 101
Clover, White, **75**
Cloudberry, 14, **15**
coal, 9
Cockle, Edible, **86**
Columbine, 17, 20, 99
Coniston Water, 106
Coot, 24, **37**, 103, 106, 108
Corby Castle, 100
Cormorant, 24, 28, **34**, 108, 111
Corn Cockle, 32
Corncrake, 31
Country Park, Bardsea, 99
Beacon Fell, 113
Talkin Tarn, 102
Witton, 117
Wycoller, 117
Cowberry, 10
Cowslip, 20, **57**
Crab, Broad-clawed Porcelain, **88**
Edible, **88**
Hermit, Common, **84**
Shore, **88**
Cranberry, 14, 26
Cranesbill, Bloody, **17**, 100, 101, 103, 106, 114
Wood, 10, 32, **32**
Creeping Jenny, **58**
Cross Fell, 5, 9, 10, 98
Crossbill, 22, **23**, 99, 108
Crow, Carrion, 22, 31, **53**
Crowberry, 14, 114
Crowfoot, Water, 26, **74**
crustaceans, **87–8**
Cuckoo, 31, **43**
Curlew, 15, 28, 31, **31**, **39**, 101, 102, 103, 113, 115, 117
Cuttlefish, Common, **88**

Dab, 30
Daffodil, Wild, 20, 99, 110
Daisy, **74**
Ox-eye, **77**
Dandelion, **61**
Deer, Fallow, 100, 106, 109
Red, **10**, 12, 23, 100, 106, 108, 109, 111
Roe, 23, **54**, 100, 101, 106, 107, 108, 109, 110, 111
Sika, 100, 109
Derwent Water, 4, 106
Dewberry, 112, 115
Dipper, 12, 26, **26**, 101, 103, 109, 110, 111, 113
Diver, Black-throated, 24
Great Northern, 24
Dock, 32
Dolphin, Bottle-nosed, 30
Dotterel, **12**
Dove, Collared, **42**
Rock, **42**
Stock, **42**
Dragonfly,
Blue, Common, 25
Golden-ringed, **25**
Hawker, Common, 15
Ischnura, Common, 25
White Faced, 26
Dropwort, 18, 99, 113
Water, 26, 116
Ducks, 24, 28, **35–6**
(see also under individual species)
Duckweed, 27
Dunlin, 15, 28, **40**, 101, 102, 115, 116
Dunnock, 31, **45**

Eagle, Golden, **12**
Eel-grass, 28
Eider, 28, **30**, 102
Elm, 20, **94**, **96**, 100
Wych, 21
Eksdale, 107
Esthwaite Water, 107

farm animals,
Appleby Castle, 99
Hornsea Pottery, 114
Lowther Wildlife Park, 109
farmland, 31
Felwort, Marsh, 106
Fern, Adder's Tongue, 116
Bracken, 13, 14, 21
Buckler, Broad, 21
Rigid, 18
Hart's Tongue, 18
Holly, 18
Lady, 21
Maidenhair, 101
Male, 21
Parsley, **13**, 110
Polypody, Common, 18
Rusty-back, 18
Wall-rue, 18
Fieldfare, 31, **48**, 112
Figwort, 26, 116
Fir, Douglas, **90**, **96**, 108, 110, 111
European Silver, **90**, **96**
Noble, 100, 110
Silver, 111
Flag, Sweet, 114
Flax, Fairy, 13
Fleabane, Blue, 99
Flycatcher, Pied, 22, 26, **47**, 99, 106, 108, 109, 111
Spotted, 22, **47**, 117
Forest, of Bowland, 6, 9, 113
Dunnerdale, 107
Ennerdale, 107
Greystoke, 100
Grizedale, 4, 22, 108
Kershope, 101
Martindale, 23
Thornthwaite, 110
Forget-me-Not, Alpine, 12
Common, **62**
Water, 25
Fox, 12, 23, 31, **54**, 108, 109, 111, 112, 113
Foxglove, **68**, 105, 106, 108, 110
Frog, 112
Fulmar, 28, **42**, 101

Gadwall, 109, 115
Gannet, 30, 102
Gardens,
Acorn Bank, 99
Brantwood, 105
Dalemain, 106
Graythwaite Hall, 108
Hesketh Park, 114
Holehird, 108
Holker Hall, 100
Hutton-in-the-Forest, 100
Levens Hall, 101
Lingholm, 109
Muncaster Castle, 109
Rusland Hall, 110
Rydal Mount, 110
Salmesbury Hall, 116
Stagshaw, 110
Whalley Abbey, 117
Garganey, 27, 115
Garlic, Wild, 113, 116, 117
Wood, **72**
Gentian, Spring, 12
Glasswort, 28, 102, 106
Globeflower, **25**, 26, 32, 105
Glow Worm, 99
Goat, Bagot, 99
Wild, 101
Godwit, Bar-tailed, 28, **39**, 102, 115
Black-tailed, **39**, 115
Goldcrest, **52**, 99, 108, 116, 117
Golden Rod, **60**, 114, 116
Goldeneye, 24, 28, 99, 108, 111, 115
Goldfinch, 31, **51**
Goosander, 24, 101, 103, 111, 115
Goose, Barnacle, 28, 102, 109
Canada, 24, **25**, **34**
Greylag, 24, **28**, 99, 107, 110, 115
Pink-footed, **28**, 99, 102, 109, 115, 116
Red-breasted, 99
White-fronted, 28, 115
Gorse, **61**
granite, 9
Grass,
Bents, 13
Cord, 28
Cotton, 14, **15**, 26, 101, 111, 113
Deer, 14
Fescue, 13
Marram, 29
Mat, 13
Moor, Blue, 17, 111
Purple, 14, 25
Nodding (Mountain Melick), 17
Quaking, Common, **17**
Wavy Hair, 21
Grass of Parnassus, 13, **29**, 32, 101, 102, 112
Grebe, 102
Great Crested, 24, **25**, **36**, 107, 111
Little, 24, **36**, 107
Red-necked, 99
Slavonian, 99
Greenfinch, **51**
Greenshank, 27, 28, **40**, 102
Groundsel, **59**
Grouse, Black, 15, **16**, 108, 113
Red, 15, **16**, 103, 113
Guillemot, 28, **42**, 101
Black, 28, 101
Gull, 30, 100, 103, 112
Black-backed, Great, 24
Lesser, **41**, 102
Black-headed, 24, 31, **41**, 102, 106, 116
Common, 24, 31, **41**
Herring, **41**, 101, 102

Haliclona oculata, **83**
Hare, Brown, 12, **55**, 112, 113
Harebell, **63**, 109
Harrier, Hen, 15, 113, 115
Marsh, 115
Hawfinch, 22, **23**, **50**
Hawthorn, Common, 20, 21, **95**, **96**, 105, 107
Hazel, **20**, 21, 105, 109, 110
Heath, Cross-leaved, 14, 26
Heather (see Ling)
Bell, **14**, **66**, 101
Hedgehog, **54**, 113
Hellebore, Green, 20, 99
Stinking, 20
Helleborine, Broadleaved, 20, 99, 112
Dark Green, 103
Dark Red, 18, **19**, 20, 99, 114
Dune, 29
Marsh, 29, 112
Helvellyn, 10
Hemlock, Western, 110
Herb Bennet, **59**
Herb Paris, 20, 21, 99, 103, 110
Herb Robert, 18, **66**, 105
Heron, 24, 108
Grey, **36**, 117
Purple, 115

Hogweed, **74**
Holly, 21, **95**, **96**, 105, 107
  Sea, 29, 102
Honeysuckle, **64**
Hoopoe, 30
Hornwort, Spineless, 101

Ice Ages, 9
Iris, Yellow, 25, 112, 113, 114, 116
Ivy, Ground, 20

Jackdaw, 31, **53**, 117
Jay, 22, **53**
Jellyfish, Moon, **87**
Juniper, 13, **20**, **91**, **96**, 111

Kestrel, 12, 22, 31, **37**
Kingfisher, **26**, **43**, 101, 116
Kittiwake, 28, **30**, 101
Knapweed, Lesser, **67**
Knot, 28, **40**, 102, 115, 116
Knotgrass, **65**

Laburnum, 116
Lady's Mantle, 32
  Alpine, 10, **11**
Lady's Smock, **67**
Lapwing, 15, 31, **38**, 102, 113, 114, 116
Larch, 21, 107, 108, 110, 111, 116
  European, **90**, **96**, 110
  Japanese, 110
Laurel, Spurge, 20, 99
Lavender, Sea, 28, **70**, 102, 106, 115
Laver, Gut, **83**
Leighton Hall, 114
Lettuce, Wall, 18
Lily of the Valley, 18, **19**, 20, 99, 110, 113, 114
Lime, Common, 20, **94**, **96**
limestone, 7, 12, 17–19, 20
  Arnside Knott, 99
  Whitbarrow, 111
limestone, Carboniferous, 8, 9, 17
limestone, Coniston, 8, 9
limestone cliffs, 28
  Humphrey Head, 100
limestone pavement, 4, 6, **18**
  Eaves Wood, 113
  Gaitbarrows NNR, 114
  Hutton Roof, 100
  Whitbarrow, 111
Limpet, Common, **85**
  Slipper, **85**
Ling, 13, 14, 17, 26, **66**
Linnet, 31, **51**, 112
Lizard, Common, 15, 108, 112
  Sand, 112
Lobelia, Water, 24, 106, 107
Lobster, Common, **88**
  Montagu's Plated, **88**
Long-tailed Duck, 28, 99
Loosestrife, Yellow, 25
Lords and Ladies, 20, **21**, 108, 117
Lousewort, 13, 102, 109

Magpie, 22, 31, **53**
Mallard, 15, 24, 28, **35**, 102, 105, 111
Marigold, Marsh, 26, 102, 103
Marten, Pine, 12, 99, 107, 110
Martin, House, 31, **44**, 103
  Sand, **44**
Martin Mere, 115
Mayweed, Scentless, 102
Meadow-rue, Alpine, 12
  Lesser, 17, 111
Meadowsweet, **31**, **74**, 101
Mercury Dog's, 18, 20, 21, **72**, 109
Mergnaser, Hooded, 99
  Red-breasted, 24, 28, **36**, 105, 106, 109, 110, 111, 115
Merlin, 15, **16**, 113, 115
Milfoil, Spiked Water, 27
Milkwort, Common, **62**, 99
  Sea, **65**, 102, 115
  Yorkshire, 102
Millstone Grit, 9
Mink, 26
Mole, 12, **54**
molluscs, **85–6**
Monkey Flower, 26
Moonwort, 17, **19**
Moorhen, 24, **37**
Morecambe Bay, 6, **28**, 115, 118
Moss, Woolly Hair, 10, **11**
  Sphagnum, 14, 25, 26, 101
Moth,
  Cinnabar, 106
  Emperor, **15**
  Green Tortrix, 23
  Least Minor, 17
  Wood Tiger, 17, **19**
  Yellow Underwing, 15
Mouse, House, 31
  Wood, 23, 31, **55**
mudflats, 4–5, 6, 28
  Bardsea, 99
  Morecambe Bay, 115
  Ribble Estuary, 6, 116
  South Solway, 102
Mullein, Great, 18
museums,
  Brantwood, 105
  Carlisle, 99
  Churchtown Botanic Gardens, 113
  Clitheroe Castle, 113
  Dalemain, 106
  Fitzpark, 107
  Hawkshead Courthouse, 108
  Haybridge, 108
  Kendal, 100
  Towneley, 117
Mussel, Common, **85**
  Horse, **86**
Mustard, Garlic, **72**
Myrtle, Bog, 26, **27**, 111

National Nature Reserve (NNR),
  Ainsdale Sand Dunes, 112
  Gaitbarrows, 18, 114
  Moorhouse, 15, 101
  Roudsea Wood, 110
National Parks,
  Lake District, 4, 5, 104–111
  Yorkshire Dales, 103
nature reserves (see also National Nature Reserve)
  Drigg Dunes, 106
  Haybridge, 108
  Healey Dell, 114
  Leighton Moss, 6, 26, 115
  Lytham St Annes, 115
  Salmesbury, 116
  Siddick Pond, 102
  South Walney, 30, 102
nature trails,
  Brantwood, 105
  Brockhole, 105
  Conishead Priory, 100
  Friars Crag, 108
  Glasson Dock, 114
  Johnny's Wood, 109
  Lancaster-Kendal Canal, 101
  Launchy Ghyll, 109
  Nether Wasdale, 109
  Poulton-le-Fylde, 116
  Roddlesworth, 116
  Rothay Valley, 109
  Squire Anderton's Wood, 117
  Stanley Ghyll, 110
  Swirls, 110
  White Moss Common, 111
Necklace Shell, **86**
Nettle, 32, **75**
  Large-flowered Hemp, 32
  White Dead, **75**
Nightjar, 111
Nightshade, Black, **78**
  Deadly, 20, 114
  Woody, 20, **70**
Nuthatch, 22, **50**

Oak, 21, 22, 23, 100, 101, 105, 106, 107, 108, 109, 110, 111, 116
  English, **91**, **96**
  Sessile, **92**, **96**, 110
Old Man's Beard, **60**
Orchid,
  Birdsnest, 20
  Butterfly, 20
    Greater, 32
    Lesser, 17, 32
  Early Marsh, 102, 112, 115
  Early Purple, 20, **69**, 99, 103
  Fly, 20
  Fragrant, 17, 32
  Frog, 17, 32
  Heath Spotted, 25, 32, 103
  Marsh, 109, 114
  Northern Marsh, 32, **32**, 102
  Small White, 32
  Spotted, 13, 32, 99
Osprey, 115
Otter, 26, **27**, **56**, 107, 115
Ouzel, Ring, **11**, 12, 101, 113
Owl, 99
  Barn, 31, **32**, 43
  Eagle, 109
  Little, 31, **43**, 102
  Long-eared, 22, **43**, 102
  Short-eared, 15, **16**, **43**, 102, 113
  Snowy, 109
  Tawny, 22, 31, **43**, 109, 114

Oyster, Common, **85**
Saddle, **85**
Oyster Plant, 29, 102
Oystercatcher, 28, 30, **38**, 102, 115, 116

Pansy, Dune, 29
Field, 32
Mountain, 103
Tricolour, 102
Wild, **61**
parkland,
Dalemain, 106
Fell Foot Park, 106
Holker Park, 100
Hornsea Pottery, 114
Leighton Hall, 115
Levens Park, 101
Lowther, 109
Rusland Hall, 110
Parsley, Cow, **73**
Upright Hedge, **73**
Partridge, 31, **37**
Pellitory-of-the-Wall, **77**
Pennine Way, 5, 98
Pennines, 9, 10, 12, 14, 118
Pennywort, Marsh, 29, 109
Peregrine Falcon, 12, **13**, 102, 107, 109, 115
Periwinkle, Common (mollusc), **85**
Flat, **86**
Periwinkle, Lesser (flower), **63**
Pheasant, **37**, 99
Pimpernel, Bog, 26
Scarlet, **71**
Yellow, **59**, 111
Wood, 21
Pine, 14, 108
Chile, **91**, **96**
Corsican, **90**, **96**, 100
Maritime, **89**, **96**
Scots, 21, **89**, **96**, 100, 107, 109, 116
Pintail, 27, 28, **35**, 100, 102, 109, 115
Pipit, Meadow, 12, 15, 17, 31, **45**
Tree, 22, **45**, 110
Plantain, Greater, **78**
Hoary, 17
Ribwort, **78**
Sea, 10
Water, 25, 27, 101, 115
Plover, Golden, 12, 15, **16**, 101, 102, 103
Grey, 28
Little Ringed, 115
Ringed, 28, 30, **38**, 102, 106, 115, 117
Pochard, 24, 27, **36**, 99, 106, 108, 109, 111
Red-crested, 99
Polecat, 99, 109
Policeman's Helmet, 26, **68**, 113
Pondweed, Bog, 14
Curly, 101
Poppy, 32
Field, **71**
Long-headed, **71**
Yellow Horned, **29**, 102, 106

Prawn, Common, **88**
Primrose, 20, **59**, 99, 103
Birdseye, 13, 32, 102, 103
Evening, 112
Puffin, 28, **42**, 101
Purslane, Pink, 114
Sea, 28, 106

Quail, 31
Quillwort, 24

Rabbit, 13, 31, **55**, 112
Ragged Robin, **67**, 103
Ragwort, **61**
Rail, Water, **27**, 115
Rape, **61**
Rattle, Yellow, **58**, 103
Raven, 12, **13**, 103, 107, 108, 109, 111, 118
Razor Shell, **86**
Razorbill, 28, **30**, 101
Redpoll, 116
Lesser, **51**
Redshank, 15, 28, **31**, **38**, 114, 115, 116, 117
Spotted, 28
Redstart, 22, **23**, **48**, 106, 108, 109, 116
Redwing, 31, **48**, 112
Reed, Common, **24**, 25
Reed-grass, 25, 27
Reedling, Bearded, 27
Reedmace, 25
Lesser, 113
Reservoir, Cow Green, **14**
Killington, 101
Stocks, 6, 117
Rest-harrow, 29, 112, 115
Rhododendron, 100, 107, 108, 109, 110, 116
Robin, 22, 31, **48**
Rocket, Sea, 29, 102, 115
Rockrose, 99
Common, 17, **19**, **58**
Hoary, 18
Rook, 31, **53**, 117
Rose, Dog, **64**
Guelder, 20, **21**
Roseroot, 10, **11**, 101
Rowan, 20, **21**, 22, **92**, **96**, 107, 109, 110, 116
Royal Society for the Protection of Birds (RSPB) reserve,
Leighton Moss, 26, 115
St Bee's Head, 101
Ruff, **40**, 115
Rush, 102
Heath, 13

St John's Wort, Common, **57**, 116
Mountain, 114
Sage, Wood, 109, 110
saltmarsh, 4–5, 6, 28
Drigg Dunes, 106
Glasson Dock, 114
Morecambe Bay, 115
Ribble Estuary, 6, 116

Saltwort, Prickly, 29, 102
Samphire, Rock, 100, 101, 102
Sand Gaper, Common, **86**
sand dunes, 4, 6, 29–30, 118
Ainsdale NNR, 112
Drigg Dunes, 106
Formby Sands, 114
Lytham St Annes, 115
South Walney, 102
Sanderling, 28, **48**, 115
Sandpier, Common, 24, 27, **38**, 101, 103, 105, 106, 108, 109, 110, 111, 113
Green, 27, 102, 115
Pectoral, 29
Wood, 27, 102, 115
Sandstone, Red, 9
Sandwort, Sea, 28, **77**
Spring, 12, 101
Sanicle, 21
Wood, 106
Saw-wort, 32
Alpine, 10
Saxifrage, Golden, 106, 113
Mossy, **10**, 101
Purple, 10, **11**
Rue-leaved, 18
Starry, 10
Yellow, 10, **11**
Scabius, 111
Devil's Bit, **69**
Field, **69**
Sheepsbit, 17
Scafell Pike, 10
Scaup, 28, 99, 115
Scoter, Common, 24, 28
Velvet, 24
Scurvy Grass, Alpine, 12
Sea Beet, **29**, 102, 115
Sea Kale, 29
Sea Lettuce, **83**
Sea Oak, **83**
Sea Potato, **87**
Sea Urchin, Edible, **87**
Seal, Common, 30, **56**
Grey, 30, **56**
seaweeds, **83**
Sedge, 26, 102
Bottle, 14
Glaucous, 17
Yellow, 110
White-beak, 27
Self Heal, 21
Shag, **34**
Shark, Basking, 30
Shearwater, 102, 114
Shelduck, 28, 30, **30**, **36**, 102, 106, 111, 114, 115
shells, **85–6**
Shephderd's Purse, **75**
shingle, 29–30
Bardsea, 99
Drigg Dunes, 106
South Walney, 106
Shoreweed, 24
Shoveler, 27, 28, **35**, 102, 109, 115
Shrew, Common, 23, **55**
Water, 26

Shrimp, Sand, **88**
White, **88**
Silverweed, **60**
Siskin, 22, **50**, 116
Skua, 30, 102, 114, 115
Skullcap, 26, 114
Skylark, 17, 31, **45**, 116
Slates, Skiddaw, 7, 9
Upper, 9
Smew, 24, 99
Snake, Grass, 108
Sneezewort, 114
Snipe, 15, 31, **40**, 101, 102
Snowberry, 100
Solomon's Seal, 99
Angular, 18, 20
Sorrel, Mountain, 10
Wood, 10, 20, **77**, 103, 108, 109, 110, 116
Sparrow, House, 31, **52**
Tree, **52**
Sparrowhawk, 22, 99, 105, 106, 111
Spearwort, 111
Speedwell, Common, **62**
Spindle, 20, 110
Spleenwort, Green, 12, 18, 101
Maidenhair, **10**, 18, 110
Sponge, Bread-crumb, **83**
Spruce, 107, 108, 111
Norway, **89**, **96**, 108, 109
Sitka, **89**, **96**, 110
Spurge, Portland, 100, 102, 106
Sea, 29, 112
Spurrey, Sand, **65**
Corn, **76**
Squinancywort, 99
Squirrel, Grey, **55**, 116
Red, **23**, **55**, 99, 105, 106, 107, 108, 109, 110, 112
Starfish, Common, **87**
Starling, **48**, 102
Starwort, Water, 24
Stint, Little, 27
Stitchwort, Common, 111
Greater, **72**
Stoat, 12, 23, 31, **56**, 113
Stonecrop, Biting, 18, **19**, 29, 102
Hairy, 101
Strawberry, Wild, **73**
Sundew, 14, **16**, 26, 102, 109
Sunstar, **87**
Swallow, 31, **44**, 102
Swan, Bewick's 102, 103, 115
Black, 99
Mute, 24, **34**, 99, 101
Whooper, 24, **25**, 102, 103, 115
Swift, 12, 31, **44**, 103
Sycamore, **94**, **96**, 105, 110, 116

tarns, 24
Sunbiggin, 102
Talkin, 103
Tarn Hows, 110
Teal, 15, 24, 28, **35**, 100, 102, 111, 115
Teasel, Wild, **69**
Tellin, Baltic, **86**
Tern, 100, 115, 118
Arctic, 30, 106
Black, 102, 115
Common, 30, **41**, 106, 116
Little, **29**, 30, **41**, 106
Roseate, 30
Sandwich, **29**, 30, 106
Thistle, Carline, 29, 106, 112, 113, 115
Melancholy, 31, **32**
Thrift, 10, **65**, 114, 115
Thrush, Mistle, 31, **49**
Song, 31, **49**
Thyme, Wild, 29
Tit, Bearded, 115
Blue, **49**
Coal, 22, **49**
Long-tailed, 22, **49**, 16
Marsh, 22, **49**, 116
Toad, Common, 112
Natterjack, **29**, 106, 112
Toadflax, Ivy-leaved, **70**
Topshell, Painted, **85**
Tormentil, **13**, 109
Touch-me-Not, **21**, 106
Treecreeper, 22, **50**, 99, 105, 108, 111, 116, 117
Trefoil, Bird's Foot, 29, **60**, 114
Trough Shell, Rayed, **86**
Tufted Duck, 24, **35**, 99, 102, 103, 106, 108, 109, 111, 115
Turnstone, 28, **38**, 115
Tutsan, 114
Twayblade, **32**
Twite, 15, 114

Ullswater, 111

Valerian, 20, 21, **68**
Vendace, 106, 108
Vetch, Horseshoe, 18
Kidney, 29, 114, 115
Milk, 100
Tufted, **70**
Violet, 103, 108
Common Dog, **69**
Dog, **17**, 109
Marsh, 111
Vole, Bank, 31
Field, 31
Short-tailed, **55**
Water, 26, **56**

waders, 28, **38–40**
Wagtail, Grey, **26**, **45**, 101, 103, 105, 109, 113, 114, 116
Pied, 26, 31, **45**
Yellow, 31, **45**
Warbler, Garden, 22, **46**
Grasshopper, 102
Icterine, 30
Reed, 27, **46**, 102, 115
Willow, 22, **46**, 109, 112
Wood, 22, **47**, 109
Water Lily, Yellow, 24, 107
White, 24, **25**, 107
Watercress, 26
Watermint, 25, 27, **69**, 101
Waxwing, 31, 99
Weasel, 12, 23, 31, **56**, 113
Wheatear, 12, 17, **18**, **47**
Whelk, Common, **85**
Dog, **85**
Netted Dog, **85**
Whimbrel, 28, **39**
Whinchat, 31, **47**
Whitebeam, 18, 20
Whitethroat, 31, **46**, 102, 112
Whiting, 30
Whitlow-grass, 29
Hoary, 17, 101
Wigeon, 28, **35**, 99, 100, 101, 102, 114, 115
Wildlife Park, Lowther, 109
Willow, 21, 25, 27, 114
Creeping, 29
Goat, **93**, **96**
Least, 10
White, **93**, **96**
Willowherb, Great, **65**, 114
Rosebay, **66**
Windermere, 4, 111
Wintergreen, Round-leaved, 29, 115
Woodcock, **22**, **39**, 108, 111, 113, 114, 116
woodland, 4–7, 20–23
(see also Forest)
Bardsea, 99
Beachwood, 99
Brock Valley, 113
Conished Priory, 100
Dodd Wood, 106
Eaves Wood, 113
Inglewood, 100
Johnny's Wood, 109
Launchy Ghyll, 109
Nether Wasdale, 109
Roudsea Wood NNR, 116
Spring Wood, 116
Squire Anderton's Wood, 117
Wetherall Woods, 103
Woodpecker, 99
Great Spotted, 22, **44**, 99, 108, 109, 111, 113, 114
Green, 22, **44**, 99, 108, 109, 111
Lesser Spotted, **44**
Woodpigeon, **42**
Sweat, 114
Woodrush, Great, 10
Woundwort, Marsh, 27
Wood, **71**
Wrack, Bladder, **83**
Channelled, **83**
Wren, 22, **46**
Wryneck, 30

Yarrow, **77**
Yellowhammer, 31, **52**
Yellow-wort, 112, 115
Yew, 20, 21, **91**, **96**, 110

zoos,
Blackpool, 113
Southport, 116

Acknowledgements: Photographers and Artists

Photographs and paintings are credited by page, from top to bottom, left to right.

Cover: Heather Angel, Denis Avon & Tony Tilford, Heather Angel, A. T. Moffett/Aquila, (painting) Chris Shields/Wilcock Riley, Paul Burnham. *Back cover:* John Sibbick/John Martin Artist.

Page 1: Walter J. C. Murray/NHPA. *Page 3:* W. F. Davidson. *Pages 4–6 (maps):* Swanston Associates. *Page 7:* Aerofilms Ltd. *Page 8 (map):* Swanston Associates. *Pages 10–11:* (painting) John Sibbick/John Martin Artists. *Page 11:* Jim Parkin, Heather Angel, C. S. Waller, Paul Burnham. *Page 12:* E. Soothill/Aquila, R. Balharny/NHPA, W. F. Davidson. *Page 13:* Heather Angel, Heather Angel, G. E. Hyde/NHPA, E. O. Fellowes, A. T. Moffett/Aquila. *Page 14:* Paul Burnham. *Page 15:* M. W. F. Tweedie/NHPA, C. S. Waller, Paul Burnham, Paul Burnham, Heather Angel. *Page 16:* George Wall, Horace Kinloch/Aquila, Malcolm Wright, R. H. Bridson, Heather Angel, R. Kennedy/Aquila, Walter J. C. Murray/NHPA. *Page 17:* R. H. Bridson, G. Preston-Mafham/NHPA. *Page 18:* R. H. Bridson, B. S. Turner. *Page 19:* R. H. Bridson, John Mason, John Mason, Heather Angel, C. S. Waller, Alida Butcher. *Page 20:* Andy Gillham, Andy Gillham. *Page 21:* John Mason, Jim Parkin, Heather Angel, B. S. Turner, Heather Angel. *Page 22:* J. F. Young, E. O. Fellowes, George Wall, *Page 23:* S. C. Bisserot, G. G. Bates/Aquila, Horace Kinloch/Aquila, E. O. Fellowes, Geoffrey Kinns. *Page 24:* John Woolverton. *Page 25:* Paul Burnham, F. J. Bingley, C. S. Waller, John Mason, Anthony Cooper/Aquila, J. F. Young. *Page 26:* E. O. Fellowes, J. F. Young, Paul Burnham. *Page 27:* G. E. Hyde/NHPA, John Mason, (painting) John Sibbick/John Martin Artists. *Page 28:* Robert Estall, N. Rodney Foster/Aquila, Joe B. Blossom/NHPA. *Page 29:* Paul Burnham, R. H. Bridson, (painting) David Hurrell/Middletons. *Page 30:* Ian C. Rose, J. Good/NHPA, John Mason, C. S. Waller, Malcom Wright. *Page 31:* Andy Gillham, J. F. Young, C. S. Waller. *Page 32:* E. O. Fellowes, Robin Fletcher, Andy Gillham, Heather Angel, Paul Burnham. *Page 33:* John Sibbick/John Martin Artists. *Pages 34–53:* Trevor Boyer. *Page 54:* Chris Shields/Wilcock Riley. *Page 55:* David Wright/Tudor Art, Chris Shields/Wilcock Riley. *Page 56:* Chris Shields/Wilcock Riley. *Pages 57–70:* Hilary Burn. *Page 71:* Hilary Burn, Michelle Emblem/Middletons, Hilary Burn. *Pages 72–78:* Hilary Burn. *Pages 79–80:* Joyce Bee. *Page 81:* Joyce Bee, Chris Shields/Wilcock Riley. *Page 82:* Joyce Bee. *Pages 83–85:* John Barber. *Page 86:* John Barber, Michelle Emblem/Middletons. *Pages 87–88:* John Barber. *Pages 89–95:* Annabel Milne & Peter Stebbing. *Page 96:* Annabel Milne & Peter Stebbing, Bob Bampton/Garden Studio (Hawthorn). *Page 97:* Colin Denwood. *Maps between pages 98 and 112:* Swanston Associates.